The Jazz o

MW01521036

leadership in a new groove

penelope tobin

DODGEM
London

Published by Dodgem
74a Woodland Gardens,
London N10 3UB
United Kingdom
E: jazzofbusiness@dodgem.org.uk

British Library Cataloguing in Publication Data
A catalogue record for this book is available from the British Library

ISBN 978-0-9565701-2-3

Produced for Dodgem by Lightning Source
Copy-edited by Sylvia Worth

Grateful acknowledgment is made to Seth Godin for permission to reproduce "Why Jazz is More Interesting Than Bowling."

to music

CONTENTS

Preface   **9**

Introduction   **15**

Where we are   16
Followers take the lead   18
Leadership for all   20
The characteristics of jazz-leadership   22

Backward Focus: Past<Self-referring   **25**

Beyond the past   27
Leaders and followers   30
Control and contribution   35
Lifelong learning   38
Solitary practice   46
Finding your voice   50
Backward Focus—Notes   53

Inward Focus: Self<Empathy   **55**

Wide view   56
Listening and responding   59
Rewarded by the groove   61
Mutually empathic   64
Soloing and comping   66
Leader/Follower   68
Stories, words and silence   73
Inward Focus—Notes   81

Downward Focus: Shadow<Trust   83

Judgement and criticism   85
Insiders and outsiders   92
Masks on friends and foes   95
Transforming mistakes   102
Trusting self and others   107
Downward Focus—Notes   111

Left Focus: Logic<Intuition   113

System meltdown   114
Motivation, goals and rewards   118
Jazz provocations and conflict   126
Improvisation   132
Control and surrender   134
Left Focus—Notes   139

Right Focus: Imagination<Structure   141

Freedom with responsibility   143
Rules and roles   150
Clarity and simplicity   157
Environment and personal space   160
Security   165
Right Focus—Notes   167

Upward Focus: Inspiration<Purpose   169

Relinquishing control   172
Purpose and passion   174
The real incentive   179

Bibliography   185

WHY JAZZ IS MORE INTERESTING THAN BOWLING

by SETH GODIN

Bowling is all about one number: the final score,

And great bowlers

    come whisker-close

        to hitting the perfect score regularly.

Not enough dimensions for me to be fascinated by,

And few people pay money to attend bowling matches.

Jazz is practised over a thousand

    or perhaps a million dimensions.

It's non-linear and non-predictable,

And most of all

    it's never perfect.

And yet

    when we get to work

        most of us choose

            to bowl.

PREFACE

Around the turn of the century I was a jazz composer, pianist and vocalist, living and working between London and New York, leading a sextet in each, composing for a 17-piece jazz orchestra, performing in clubs most nights, frequently teaching and running workshops by day, as well as touring in Europe and Japan. *The Jazz of Business* is the reaction of that world colliding with the one I unexpectedly entered…

I became curious about the barriers to creativity, and began to research the difference between how we 'access' our innate soft skills such as creativity, as opposed to how our education systems 'input' the hard skills of knowledge and technical aptitude into us. Emerging from this study was the relationship between twenty-first century skills needs and the artist's way of working (being artists of all disciplines). What had once been seen as a maverick lifestyle, full of uncertainty, is becoming increasingly mainstream; having always worked this way, the artist is very effective at it, while others, encountering it for the first time and only having been provided with skills input by education systems, are ill-equipped to cope, and are suffering as a result. I felt sure that the artist's way of working would point towards a more relevant approach, one that would allow us to develop the skills demanded by our new circumstances.

To put my findings into practice I founded Barrier Breakers, a charity to help troubled young people build their potential and improve their lives, and discovered that the approach I used (BBM) was extremely effective. Since those early days, BBM has been tried, tested, and used successfully in an ever-increasing number of research, evaluation, training and consultancy contexts, helping individuals and organisations to identify and break down barriers, so they can access and develop their inherent soft skills capabilities. This fascinating work has drawn me in, insisting that I pay full attention to it—and, having seen the value that BBM generates in terms of both well-being and bottom-line results, I'm willingly at its service.

However, *The Jazz of Business* brings me back to where I started this journey, and also back to what makes my heart sing—to jazz. After a decade of exploration into the artist's way of working, I'm convinced that the jazz-leader provides the best model for all those who have to lead within entirely new, turbulent circumstances, who need to build structures that have both the strength and the flexibility to contain uncertainty, who must create environments that allow the individual to flourish while collaborating with others on a common purpose, and who need to innovate, to inspire, and, above all, to improvise. This book presents this kind of leadership—leadership in a new groove, or jazz-leadership.

The characteristics of jazz-leadership are framed here within BBM—or Barrier Breakers Methodology for Soft Skills Development and Evaluation:

Soft skills are the traits and abilities of attitude and behaviour rather than knowledge or technical aptitude.

BBM is a mechanism of six 'lenses' that reveal where these soft skills—such as communication, innovation, empathy, self-motivation, and collaboration—are being blocked, and the means through which they're overcome—in this case, by jazz-leadership. I've described each of the lenses—or Barrier Profiles—at the beginning of the relevant chapter, but for a more comprehensive explanation, visit www.barrierbreakers.co.uk or read *Barrier Breakers: Be Yourself Brilliantly!*

"Soft" stuff rules—everything derives from the "soft" stuff.
TOM PETERS

Quotes are from exemplary jazz and business leaders, and while not every great leader could be included here—and some of your favourites are no doubt missing—I hope your interest will be piqued by the unfamiliar names, and you'll be moved to explore their work, words, and music.

And I must apologise to grammar pedants; instead of using 'his' or 'her' I've chosen to use 'their'—breaking rules sometimes just makes sense!

Few things are as difficult for an organisation as transforming from one kind of team to another. This demands the most difficult learning imaginable: unlearning.

PETER DRUCKER

Writing this book has been immensely interesting, pleasurable and enlightening. Having been immersed in business leadership over recent years, it was fascinating to turn my attention to the experiences and personal perspectives of the jazz-leaders whose music I love—music that is the soundtrack to this book. I found profound wisdom in their words, which time and again made the link to leadership an easy task for me, along with a harmony in their perceptions that gave depth to my premise. As an added benefit, my own journey as both jazz musician and leader has been enriched and informed in ways that I hadn't anticipated at the outset. I hope that you'll be as inspired by these jazz-leaders as I have been, and that by the end of reading you'll be fully in the 'groove' of jazz-leadership.

INTRODUCTION

I used to think that running an organization was equivalent to conducting a symphony orchestra. But I don't think that's quite it; it's more like jazz. There is more improvisation.

WARREN BENNIS

W e're living in a frenzy of change, old regimes toppling, financial systems collapsing, borders being literally and virtually broken down, and new technology in every nook and cranny of our lives. Change is constant. And this means we all have to get good at improvising (from the Latin "improvises," meaning "not seen ahead of time").

Improvisation is playing extemporaneously ... composing on the spur of the moment.

GUNTHER SCHULLER

To navigate this uncharted territory we need leaders who understand how to establish the best structures for uncertainty, who adapt to change in real time, who learn continuously, and who inspire others to co-create their vision of the future. The authoritarian individual, working to a fixed, detailed plan from a detached position of control, is ill-equipped to deal with our new circumstances.

If the old leadership paradigm looked like the conductor of an orchestra, the new one can be seen as the leader of a jazz group—a jazz-leader. This is leadership in a new groove.

Jazz is a very democratic art form. This is a collective; you learn from everybody.

MAX ROACH

WHERE WE ARE

We're being confronted by multiple complex issues that are reshaping our lives and, simultaneously, technology is changing everything about being human. That we're now globally connected is game-changing in and of itself, but then new media is altering the very nature of how we communicate; smart machines and systems force us to question what it means to be human; emerging industry structures send our concept of an organisation spinning;

computerisation turns life into data; increasingly available information about everything and everybody makes us more informed, more transparent, more manipulated, more vulnerable. When these technologically-driven upheavals are seen in the context of emerging global issues, such as the ageing population in developed economies, increased demand for declining natural resources, and geopolitical instability, it's clear that challenges are growing exponentially. Leaders are facing an abundance of complexity never before encountered, and, consequently, the look of leadership must change.

We are experiencing a demand for new types of skills and sacrifices in C-level executives that many are not prepared to bring to the table.
TOM NEFF

Around the world, this rapid change is going hand in hand with a loss of faith in leadership. We're emerging from a time when most leaders controlled through coercion, charisma, or by demanding compliance to a tradition, generally for reasons of self-aggrandisement rather than for the good of their people. In democracies, as in autocracies, the tide is turning away from traditional forms of leadership, and every day more questions are being asked of leaders, more doubts are being shared and expressed by more societies, and the realisation is dawning that not only have many in power been abusing their position and their people, but they are also insufficiently skilled to lead in such a chaotic environment.

We have a crisis of confidence in this country. Washington is not producing the leadership we need and it is time that corporations and business leaders realise that we too have to do something.

HOWARD SCHULTZ

As followers wake up to this reality, and disillusion in the old power structures grows, what emerges is an urgent need for a new understanding of leadership, and for a radically different kind of leader.

The hierarchical approach—let's just lead from the top and if other people don't like it, that's their problem—does not work anymore. You've got to engage with multiple constituencies and make decisions in a more consensual way.

JOHN BROCK

FOLLOWERS TAKE THE LEAD

Followers, not leaders, are heading up change. In general, leaders are disinclined to admit their deficiencies, alter their approach, or share power. Although some courageous and forward-looking business leaders already recognise that their role must change in response to circumstances, many more will find it hard to move to a new model, particularly if they fear they'll personally lose power and prestige, or if their skills were learnt through traditional management education or leadership-development experiences. There's evidence that having become accustomed to a command and control mindset many business leaders are reverting to this in crisis mode.

It is very hard when you are inside one paradigm, to really visualise a different one.

IAN CHESHIRE

Consequently, it's followers, not leaders, who must determine what the new face of leadership will look like. Traditional leadership has evolved from a primarily aggressive standpoint, and this still informs our predominant expectations of a leader. Will followers continue to be persuaded by the manipulative or wooed by the charismatic, silenced by authority or cowed through fear? Or will they question their understanding of both leadership and followership? Leaders and followers alike have to question how the accepted leadership paradigm has affected us all, and whether this is the path we want to continue along. What do we expect a leader to look like, to sound like, and to behave like? Do we feel that our assumptions have delivered us with the best leaders? If not, what would great leadership look like? How would it work from the global perspective or within the team dynamic, as a corporate driver or as an entrepreneurial motivator? Do we believe that the current leadership model is healthy for all people and is appropriately skilled to guide us through the chaos of a rapidly changing, interconnected, unstable world? If not, then we have to change a long-held understanding of what leadership and followership are, in order to get—or to be—the leaders we need now.

Innovation leaders are different. People who have been successful in the past might not have the mindset or talent for it.

A.G. LAFLEY

LEADERSHIP FOR ALL

Leadership is no longer the rarefied dominion of those at the top of vast institutions; it's the concern of everyone. Along with increased instability have come greater freedom, more choice, and a responsibility to carve our own destinies. Unshackled from predictability, we've found ourselves thrown into the mêlée of constant flux, and forced to manage ourselves and lead others to a far greater extent than at any other time. As career paths become more erratic, financial security less common, and the job for life is confined to history, we each have to take charge of designing our lives, and become more at home with uncertainty. Either we'll end up as flotsam on the tide of change, or we'll find a way to navigate it successfully.

The probability of serious innovation coming from big companies over the mid- to long-term is very low.
TOM PETERS

Patterns of work are shifting, and new kinds of followers and leaders are emerging. For example, by 2011 the ranks of the self-employed in the UK had swelled to a record 4.1 million—14.2 per cent of all employed people, according to the Office for National Statistics. Yet this increasingly common way of working is still regarded as something of an anomaly in the workforce. There is a growing number of people who choose to run their own small businesses, rather than work for somebody else, and these 'alterpreneurs' represent a different breed of entrepreneur—they have no interest in being a tycoon and building a global empire, but are looking to carve out an alternative to traditional employment; they are not concerned with the accumulation of wealth or power, but with a good quality of life. For them leadership is not about controlling a multi-billion dollar enterprise and thousands of employees, but about having the necessary vision and skills to bring a small, often disparate group along with them—maybe comprising a few employees, a web of freelance associates, some remote workers, a network of contacts, suppliers, and clients. And it's inevitable that among those they 'lead', there are many who lead their own groups, their own networks, in a similar way.

Extended enterprises are creating new forms of webbed businesses, based on collaboration and driven by relationships, requiring a new style of leadership, not just from a single CEO, but from people throughout organisations of all shapes and sizes.

Success is now the domain of people who lead. That doesn't mean they're in charge, it doesn't mean they are the CEO, it merely means that for a group, even a small group, they show the way, they spread ideas, they make change. Those people are the only successful people we've got.

SETH GODIN

THE CHARACTERISTICS OF JAZZ-LEADERSHIP

Jazz-leadership is based on commonalities shared by all jazz idioms, at the heart of which is the ability to work successfully with improvisation. The term 'jazz-leadership' derives from jazz, but it is not limited to that setting. It embodies a particular set of characteristics—applicable to any leadership context—that fall within themes explored in *The Jazz of Business,* including:

Primary themes:

- rotating leadership and followership
- achieving individuality within collaboration
- managing risk while encouraging innovation
- co-creating a vision—the idea in the middle
- building structures for improvisation
- achieving the groove.

Secondary themes:

- motivation, engagement, commitment
- lifelong and multi-level learning
- constructive provocation and conflict
- empathic communication
- genuine diversity
- transforming mistakes
- effective reward systems
- culture of trust
- valuing process
- purpose and meaningful work.

Everything rises and falls on leadership.

JOHN MAXWELL

CHAPTER I

Backward Focus: Past<Self-referring

Backward focus has the dominant influence of the past. In a positive sense, the past allows us to use experience as the basis for current action, to draw from tradition, to be rooted in a culture. In jazz, tradition plays an important role; understanding the roots of the music, historically and theoretically, is at the heart of any jazz apprenticeship.

Some groups are based around a particular idiom, and will abide by its conventions, and those of the various styles within it; others blend different elements to produce something new. Knowing these conventions is essential in order to participate, and musicians are judged on their ability to understand, play within, and move on from established traditions. Gerry Mulligan expressed this as not a revolution against a dead regime, but a natural evolution, with respect shown to its ancestry.

However, if backward focus takes over, and the past has too much influence, it becomes a barrier. This causes an individual or organisation to be conformist, to lack flexibility, to be constrained within what they know, to play it safe and resist change, to draw from others just enough to reflect current trends but to offer little that is new themselves.

For an improviser, being derivative is always of concern—how much one draws on tradition, or one's own repertoire of 'licks,' has to balance with experimentation, change, and risk-taking.

My greatest fear is the fear of not being able to go along with change, of becoming stylistic and set.

HENRY THREADGILL

Jazz-leadership breaks through the barrier of backward focus by using self-referring approaches, to move beyond the past, know one's own values, be self-aware and self-reliant, learn constantly, and find one's own voice.

Anything you are shows up in your music—jazz is whatever you are, playing yourself, being yourself, letting your thoughts come through.

MARY LOU WILLIAMS

BEYOND THE PAST

You have to know where you came from in order to know where you're going.

LOUIE BELLSON

When we experience an uncertain environment—such as improvisation—there's a tendency to try to control it; unfortunately, this has the counterproductive effect of shutting down creativity and innovation. Richard Foster calls it 'cultural lock-in'—the stiffening of the invisible architecture and ossification of mental models and decision-making processes. Margaret Wheatley, organisational behaviour expert, has observed that business leaders are reverting to command and control in response to current upheavals. They've defaulted to what they know, even if it's outmoded and ineffective as a response. While current circumstances would be better addressed by new, more democratic approaches that encourage innovation, Wheatley believes that senior executives are under the illusion that by taking power back to the top they can manage the crisis effectively.

When we try and control chaos all we do is create more chaos.

MARGARET WHEATLEY

It's easy to slide into the familiar, but it's a response driven by habit or fear rather than vision. Jazz-leaders work *with* uncertainty. They use it to inspire people to stretch themselves, to challenge limitations, to question assumptions about what's possible. Thelonius Monk, for example, would insist that his players went beyond what he saw as the artificial boundaries of convention they'd absorbed, in terms of what they believed could be produced on their instrument. While for Steve Lacy, jazz is "something to do with the 'edge'—always being on the brink of the unknown and being prepared for the leap."

Backward focus can be promulgated by forces external to an individual or organisation—in the jazz world this could be the audience demanding old favourites rather than unfamiliar work, or critics becoming hostile if a musician's style changes over time. Pat Matheny sees this as affecting musicians "on a profound level—that's how you're defined within the musical community, by what 'style' you play." It takes courage to step beyond the familiar, to defy what others expect of you, to change.

Every time you change you have to be ready to experience massive rejection.
JONI MITCHELL

But it's this kind of change that's needed in leadership behaviour. We're navigating uncharted territory that's throwing challenges at us we've never encountered before. Leaders have to improvise, which means drawing on tradition and experience but moving away from it—completely rejecting it if that's what is called for. If organisations don't dare to leave it all behind, they could meet the same fate as Kodak, the 133-year old business that, despite being at the forefront of digital photography, failed to make the necessary leap into the new market, and was overtaken.

Duke Ellington is continually renewing himself through his music. He's thoroughly attuned to what's going on now. He not only doesn't live in the past, he rejects it.

BILLY STRAYHORN

Overcoming backward focus is achieved by moving beyond limitations that have been absorbed through the past, such as personal experience, culture, tradition, or societal assumptions. It requires a deep understanding of who you are and what you wish to achieve, and the self-determination to head in that direction, even though it may be going against the tide. Tony Hsieh built Zappos in a new way, by putting company culture above everything else, and believing—correctly—that this would lead to superlative customer service. Rather than sell his company purely on the basis of financial profit, he waited until he was certain that the deal he struck with Amazon ensured that the Zappos culture would remain. His vision was so strong—"Zappos wasn't just a job, it was a calling"—that it directed the choices he made, and determined how he did things differently. This self-referring process is essential for anyone who wants to find their own voice, develop their vision, forge their path, believe in it enough to make decisions based upon it, and then bring others along; it's at the core of jazz-leadership.

Leadership is the ability to transform vision into reality.
WARREN BENNIS

LEADERS AND FOLLOWERS

The need for new leadership goes hand in hand with the need for new followership. But just as chaos causes leaders to revert to the familiar, followers too can hit the barrier of backward focus. This barrier stops questions being asked, demands compliance, limits self-reliance, kills initiative. The lure of backward focus is the comfort of the familiar, the security of the status quo, the promise of being taken care of, the excuse of 'this is the way it's always been done,' the ease of a life defined by another's dogma. Those making change need to be constantly vigilant, or they're likely to find the old ways have 'snuck' back in and re-established themselves. Only when followers recognise and reject old models can new followership, and consequently new leadership, emerge.

The position of the follower is always underrated. The band has to have great followers; you can't have five great leaders.

BRANFORD MARSALIS

Followership is paid far less attention than leadership. Few studies have been done on the subject, and it's neither fully valued, nor is its complexity understood. A follower is generally seen in negative terms, and associated with qualities such as passivity, lack of imagination, and low personal drive—perhaps reflecting the way followership has evolved in the culture of command and control leadership. Consequently, followership is not a trait that's encouraged, and receives no professional development attention. But every group has to have great followers, and followership has its own skills, which are integral to, and encouraged by, jazz-leadership.

Followers who tell the truth, and leaders who listen to it, are an unbeatable combination.

WARREN BENNIS

The barrier of backward focus is broken through in an environment where the individual—leader or follower—is able to self-refer, to speak the truth as they see it, to work according to their own values system, to pursue personal growth. The significance of this to both the individual's satisfaction and to performance and productivity has been proven in recent research, such as that undertaken by Teresa Amabile. This has shown the link between the bottom line, and what Amabile terms 'inner work life'—the emotions, perceptions and motivations that people experience as they react and try to make sense of their work life. Of all events that deeply engage people, the single most important one is making progress on work that they find meaningful, in which they find a sense of purpose. When the motivation is intrinsic, rather than external, then the effect is most profound.

Better inner work life for employees yields tangible benefits for companies, their customers, and their shareholders.

TERESA AMABILE

As well as showing the reasons for top performance, and its relationship to employee engagement and business success, Amabile's research also provides evidence that business leaders tend to be unaware of the power of intrinsic motivation, and expend their energies with employees on less impactful areas. By contrast, the jazz-leader understands that you must engage someone in order to get their best work, and to do this you need to provide an environment that gives each individual the opportunity to reach for their own personal goals, while moving everyone in the same direction. This simple formula elicits optimum individual and collective performance.

You got to study each man in the band, because each has a different disposition. Actually, you got to use a lot of psychology because they all have different temperaments and habits.

EARL HINES

Once personnel have been chosen, the jazz-leader is completely focused on how to make the most of each individual's strengths. While this involves a consideration of the well-being and development of everyone concerned, there is an entirely pragmatic purpose behind it—the individual and the collective feed off each other, benefiting the group and the overall performance.

A leader's role is to maximise strengths so that weaknesses become irrelevant.

PETER DRUCKER

What this means in practice is, for example, that Keith Jarrett will tailor his composing to fit those in his current group. For him, the hardest part of writing is to make it a personal statement for everyone involved; substitute any one musician, and the music written would be different. Similarly, when Bill Evan's bassist, Scott LaFaro, was killed in a car crash, Evans knew that despite LaFaro's replacement being "a strong, intelligent, and accomplished talent in himself," he could not duplicate the point of development that the trio had reached by that point. It was "a different trio now." This sensitivity to the individual's impact on the whole is echoed in Ellington's compositional approach. He used the unique qualities of his musicians as inspiration, working with their idiosyncrasies rather than trying to adapt them, and producing pieces that played to the inherent attributes of each player.

You write just for their abilities and natural tendencies and give them places where they do their best.

DUKE ELLINGTON

According to work by Rath and Conchie, this 'strengths' approach lifts employee engagement from 9 per cent to 73 per cent, while similarly dramatic results are evident in a study of 90,000 employees by the Corporate Leadership Council, which showed that an emphasis on performance strengths was linked to a 36 per cent improvement in performance, whereas an emphasis on weaknesses—the more common management approach—was linked to a 27 per cent decline.

Because the individual's strengths are recognised, and their contribution has a place and purpose, the jazz-leader is rewarded by a genuine commitment from everyone in the group, to the group; meanwhile, the part each member plays within the ensemble resonates with them, and they know that they're valued for exactly what they have to offer.

CONTROL AND CONTRIBUTION

When a leader has a clear and compelling vision, it's not always easy for them to work with a consensual approach, and frequently there's tension between maintaining the vision and allowing others to influence it, between the ideals of personal self-expression and collective contribution.

> *At times I have to fight not to tell anyone else how to play. It might not be what I had in mind, but that's the whole point of playing jazz, to be open enough to accept what someone else has to say.*
>
> FRED HERSCH

Jazz-leaders balance their need to maintain control, to hold the vision, and to steer the direction, with the need to ensure that each musician's contribution is adding something, otherwise "they may feel that they're a deadweight in the band—just holding an instrument and not serving a real function," says Herbie Hancock; "the personality of the individual players must be present in the music."

> *Everyone has to follow the leader's concept, but add everything they can to it.*
>
> WYNTON MARSALIS

Getting the best from people is good for everyone, but the factors that stimulate this are often overlooked by business leaders; rather there tends to be a *demand* that people should do their best. However, we all perform according to context. It's the leader's responsibility to select the appropriate personnel, to create and monitor the best environment for peak performance, to consistently exhibit a genuine conviction that everyone's contribution is important, and to tailor their leadership approach to suit both the individuals and the situation.

Betty Carter provides a good example of 'situational leadership'—a theory developed by Paul Hersey and Ken Blanchard—in her ability to adapt her leadership behaviour to suit the specific needs of the situation. She would seek out and nurture talented young players, overseeing their progress. But she didn't carry the relational behaviour into the performance, where her demeanour was unambiguously directive, entirely focused on driving performance up. This kind of leadership behaviour is powerfully motivating, and leads to high competence plus high commitment.

Betty Carter expects a serious contribution from everybody and draws it out of them. She gets right in your face when she sings. It's real communication. It's a real band.

DAVE HOLLAND

While drawing out the individual's voice is good for the individual concerned and for the collective, it does involve elements of risk for the leader. For example, maintaining the overall vision is more difficult when some power is transferred, as in a collaborative improvisation. However, doing this reflects a confidence not only in the followers' abilities, but also in the leader's capacity to select the right people—those who are capable of carrying a vision, who provide the skills that the leader themselves lack, who understand their role, and who will do the job well. Mark Zuckerberg took this idea a little further. In 2007 he set up a recruitment process that involved Facebook's rank-and-file engineers identifying candidates—by going on campus visits and attending meetups—and then interviewing them. Zuckerberg's confidence in his team's abilities not only to do their jobs, but also to select their peers, paid off.

The compositional act of choosing players doesn't always work out as intended, with skills mismatches, direction disagreements, and personality clashes emerging over time. Charles Mingus admitted that his attempts weren't always successful, and musicians could get caught up in the music and go in their own direction, rather than the one he intended them to work on. But the jazz-leader understands this. It's their challenge to hold their vision steady despite eruptions, to allow freedom but know when and how to pull it back into the collective vision if it strays too far. In order to be comfortable with others' contribution, to view collaboration as an asset not a threat, the jazz-leader has complete conviction about their vision and stays true to their core values.

With this, they can be clear about pointing the way. As Carlos Santana said of Miles Davis, "we all benefit from his courage to embrace the future full on."

Miles Davis is a leader in jazz because he has definite confidence in what he likes and he is not afraid of what he likes. He has confidence in his own taste and he goes his own way.

GIL EVANS

LIFELONG LEARNING

Jazz-leaders actively encourage individual development, enthusing if leaders emerge from the ranks of their groups. But in many organisations anything that could accelerate employee 'churn' is seen as a risk to be avoided. A familiar argument against employee training is that it's counterproductive and a waste of money—by upskilling employees they'll grow out of their position more quickly and move on; knowledge learnt at the expense of the organisation will become an advantage for a competitor. However, training can be used as a way of attracting high-quality candidates—for example, in response to the growing leadership gap, organisations that provide excellent leadership development programmes will not only be able to nurture existing talent, but will also bolster the company's offering when competing for new hires.

Unilever's Leadership Development Programme prepares our future leaders for an increasingly volatile and uncertain world where the only true differentiation is the quality of leadership.

PAUL POLMAN

The jazz-leader sees learning as a continuum, moving out of the tradition, affected by personal experience, intimately linked to the individual 'voice' and benefiting the whole. Employee turnaround is a necessary part of this process, bringing with it new ideas and fresh collaborations.

Learning is not compulsory ... neither is survival.

W. EDWARDS DEMING

Learning has changed for everyone—the when, what, why, where, how of learning is not as it was, even in the recent past. Most education was designed for a different time and purpose, our studying limited to our youth, when we'd assimilate the bulk of the information that was necessary to carry us through our lives. But now, to keep abreast of change, we need to learn different skills, and we need to keep learning throughout our lives, which are longer than ever. This learning is often, and increasingly, down to the individual. A sole trader or small business-owner must identify their own learning needs. They have to evaluate their own strengths and weaknesses; research and source the appropriate training; fund it themselves; sacrifice earnings while they undertake it; integrate their new learning into their work; and assess their progress. This process, already familiar to many freelance practitioners, is the way of the jazz-leader, and is becoming increasingly common.

It's taken me all my life to learn what not to play.
DIZZY GILLESPIE

So our learning is up to us, and is lifelong—nobody directs it for us, it doesn't necessarily take place in an education institution, and we don't always receive qualifications for it. We need information, but, more crucially, we need to be adept at selecting the information we need, and then at making connections between that information. We have to come up with the questions and the answers ourselves. This is the self-referring behaviour that moves us beyond backward focus. While we learn from the past in its many forms, if we stay focused on it rather than examining it and moving beyond it, then we're not doing the learning we need for today's world.

Music has a tradition that you have to understand before you can move to the next step. But that doesn't mean you have to be a historian.
WYNTON MARSALIS

Despite the need for lifelong learning, research shows that many top executives rarely or never discuss their personal or team development, or only cover it as an annual formality. A survey of 350 U.S. companies by Ashridge Business School showed that their development is "perfunctory, haphazard and uncoordinated," and suggests that the gap between skills requirements and leader capability is growing. The report concluded that this is "shocking," and the situation needs to be shaken up with an approach that is "courageous, creative, and both systematic and systemic." The jazz-leader's attitude to lifelong learning, the way they model this to their followers, and the link between individual and business development, provides a model of good practice.

Try, fail, learn. Try, fail, learn. Try, fail, learn. That's the leader's mantra. Leaders are learners.

JIM KOUZES

While jazz is now represented in formal education, earlier leaders learnt in an entirely different way. Some think that the formalisation of learning has been to the detriment of jazz, that it provides knowledge without wisdom, information without experience, technique without depth, and it removes elements from the learning process that are vital to the development of a unique voice.

Universities are good for general knowledge, but they really don't do this job of creating freedom. Most people that go to these universities don't really start playing until two or three years after they get away from them.

ANDREW HILL

That jazz is a music derived solely from an untrained 'feel', a spontaneous outpouring of innate musicality, is a vastly inaccurate, yet curiously widespread fallacy. Before the availability of jazz education programmes, musicians were still schooled—some had formal classical training, others learnt the basics informally from family and friends. However, when it came to jazz learning, all jazz musicians had to structure and undertake their own journey. Perhaps this in part explains its reputation as music of the untutored; rather, it is an example of the kind of demanding, self-directed learning we need today.

Whether the jazz musician has been through formal education or not, their learning will still bear similarities to that of past jazz masters—a process that includes undertaking their own research and investigation, rigorous solitary practice, listening to elders, observing performers 'in-action', jam sessions, 'sitting-in' on other people's gigs, working with peers, listening to and analysing recordings, as well as seeking out and entering into dialogue with musical mentors. This multi-level learning experience has no pre-determined curriculum, graduation date or qualification—as Eartha Kitt said, "I am learning all the time. The tombstone will be my diploma." The learning is intrinsically motivated, and is achieved through, and therefore develops, extraordinary dedication, motivation and persistence. Consequently, each unique learning journey becomes the catalyst that produces a particular voice, shaping the individual, personally and as a musician.

The thing that makes jazz so interesting is that each man is his own academy.
CECIL TAYLOR

Many musicians talk about their 'apprenticeships'—the groups within which they developed not only their 'chops', or musical fluency, but also the capacity to cope with the day-to-day reality of being a working musician, including the practicalities of jazz performance. Unpredictable working conditions are extremely challenging at any time in a career, but particularly for the novice. And this is a working environment that is consistently uncertain; there are numerous technical and practical variables that affect performance, from the acoustics of the venue, to the different types of audience; problems with sound systems, or poor quality pianos. For the sake of overall performance and personal well-being, the jazz-leader learns to be extremely flexible and adaptive, not just in order to undertake the work itself, but also to cope effectively with the conditions under which the work takes place. Until quite recently this would have been considered unusual, but constant unpredictability within the workplace is becoming increasingly common in all walks of life.

One of the things I learned with Dizzy's band was how to be consistent in my playing, how to play the best I could every night, no matter what the odds, no matter what the circumstances.

KENNY BARRON

Marian McPartland was already a professional musician when she felt her apprenticeship really started, when she learnt about the kind of accompaniment different musicians liked to hear behind them, how to relate to an audience, how to treat the sidemen, and so on. These apprenticeships were as tough as anything that could be provided by an institution, and generations of musicians have used metaphors of formal education to describe the training they received. Red Rodney described his experience with Charlie Parker as "like going to college and graduate school all at once," while Walter Bishop Jr. believed that "playing with each group is a formal education."

Art Blakey's band, *The Jazz Messengers*, was the academy for numerous musicians who went on to become leaders. Under his mentorship, players such as Wynton Marsalis were encouraged to develop sufficiently to leave, or 'graduate,' and become leaders in their own right. This kind of mentor–leader is a familiar jazz model, with Betty Carter being another who believed passionately in her role as educator, in preparing young musicians not only for leadership, but also—and firstly—for followership.

Education is very important to me. Everybody can't be a leader. Everybody can't be a star.

BETTY CARTER

Much jazz-learning takes place with colleagues, in 'communities of practice.' Dexter Gordon said that his conversations about improvisation went on with Illinois Jacquet constantly, "everyday, on the bus, off the bus, in the hotel, on the stand." And for Roy Haynes, "every time I have a discussion with musicians I always learn something." Sonny Rollins acknowledges that "in a way I was self-taught, but I got a lot of help along the way from a lot of senior guys." In the manner of a true apprenticeship, Rollins learnt from listening and being around more experienced players, from picking things up, and from "always thinking of getting better."

This kind of learning rarely happens in today's organisations, although the complexity of our current situation calls for it more than ever. But finding time to explore best solutions, reflect on action, and learn together is seldom made a priority.

We've become task processors, rather than thoughtful human beings.

MARGARET WHEATLEY

Some forward-looking organisations recognise the value of capturing and sharing the wealth of wisdom in their people. IBM has used the possibilities that social media offers, encouraging their 320,000 employees to start blogs and creating a wiki so the bloggers themselves could develop guidelines for navigating the blogosphere. Now, as well as collaborating internally via an intranet, 'IBMers' share their work, learn, and gain feedback from customers, partners, and competitors.

SOLITARY PRACTICE

Although these communities of practice and apprenticeships are essential to jazz learning, the work of understanding the language of jazz begins and ends with the individual. It is entirely the individual's responsibility not only to undertake the learning, but also to identify their learning needs, and design their learning programme. Charlie Parker's apprenticeship period was concluded on his own; he took himself away for months to 'woodshed' after coming face to face with musical flaws that disturbed him. Recognised eventually as an innovative genius, Parker, like all jazz musicians, had to work extremely hard on his own to find himself musically.

Music is an art, and art has its own rules. And one of them is that you must pay more attention to it than anything else in the world, if you're going to be true to yourself. And if you don't do it – and you are an artist – it punishes you.

NINA SIMONE

For musicians, practice isn't finite, or even something that happens occasionally as a top-up; practice is a constant. Often done on a daily basis, practice involves self-assessment, goal setting, metacognition, and self-evaluation; it's a targeted, precise and deliberate activity. While some research claims that it takes ten years of practice to reach master-level performance, practice continues throughout a musician's career, irrespective of the level they achieve. Wynton Marsalis, for example, is "still trying to understand certain things." He knows that he'll never arrive at the place he wants to be. It's not a race against others, but a means of developing his own potential. He's an example of the intrinsically motivated jazz-leader, who believes that "you practice and you develop throughout your entire life to as high a level as you can get to."

I practice every day. I'm thinking music all the time anyway. I've always been learning. I think that I'm still learning. At least I hope I am, because music is endless, you can always learn something.

SONNY ROLLINS

Jazz musicians are concerned not only with maintaining their technique and expanding their repertoire, but also with their fluency in the language of improvisation. While the former are time consuming it's the latter in particular that entails a never-ending exploration, aptly described by Michel Petrucciani:

> *Sometimes I'm practising and I have to define something. I get to the door, and I open it, and the work that is there behind that door is unbelievable. Then eventually I get through cleaning that up, and open another door and there's something even bigger. And it never, never ends.*
>
> MICHEL PETRUCCIANI

This endeavour of solitary exploration is an intellectual process that's undertaken so that the rules and theory are integrated, so the musician can learn and dissect the material, and understand how to work with it. And then "it takes years and years of playing to develop this facility, so you can forget all that, and just relax and play," said Bill Evans. This kind of continuous self-directed learning is essential for all leaders, and, as the pace of change accelerates, is ever more so.

> *Just because you are CEO, don't think you have landed. You must continually increase your learning, the way you think, and the way you approach the organization.*
>
> INDRA NOOYI

A leader cannot make the best decisions unless they've first assimilated the facts—which need constant renewal—and then collected the current 'material' so it can be understood and dissected, and their options are fully revealed. After which they need the courage to relinquish the intellectual control, and allow their instinct to come to the fore, working freely from the foundation of all that accrued learning.

> *Have the courage to follow your heart and intuition. They somehow already know what you truly want to become. Everything else is secondary.*
> STEVE JOBS

A jazz-leader is always open to new ideas, and humble enough to admit, like George Benson, that "I'm hearing new things all the time. I'm always saying, 'why didn't I ever think of that?'" Or Joe Sample, at the peak of his profession and having been a pianist for 42 years, yet able to admit that there was so much more to learn.

> *It just keeps going on and on and on and on. You're in that constant state of being a student.*
> JOE SAMPLE

The jazz-leader in any business understands that learning is an open-ended process, a continuous unfolding not a finished product. They're comfortable with 'the more you know, the less you understand,' and the paradox doesn't impinge on their desire to question, investigate and seek to improve their performance. Behind every decision they make, just as behind every idea that an improviser unfurls, there's a lifetime of preparation and knowledge.

Great leaders reinvent continuously on a personal level ... the very best leaders are learners.

KEN BLANCHARD

FINDING YOUR VOICE

This approach to learning requires personal drive and inner resources to be ignited by a compelling vision, and an insistent curiosity to be fuelled by a purpose. Without these, the enormity of the endeavour would be too daunting and impatience would win; with these, the process is a fascinating exploration.

The main thing I like about what I'm trying to do is that I know that it's impossible.

MOSE ALLISON

For the jazz musician, the driving force behind the relentless exploration is to get closer to their own voice, to have the facility to express themselves unencumbered by any technical limitations, to "tell the truth as I see it," says Wynton Marsalis. Similarly for his brother, Branford, the unravelling of his personal journey is the primary motivator, "I do my records for me … it's my own personal growth process."

Playing with people who are their own players taught me how to find myself.
JOE LOVANO

In a crowded, competitive environment, the way an individual or organisation can differentiate themselves is to have their own distinctive style, to be authentic, and speak in their own voice. The time comes for any leader when they've formulated their vision, when they've found their voice, when they're being innovative. At this point they have to consider how they should be affected by feedback they receive—to assess whether it's valuable and will sustain their vision, or whether it's merely one opinion among many.

Imitate, assimilate, innovate.
CLARK TERRY

The jazz-leader begins playing like someone else; they imitate. Then they learn the craft, gather information, dissect their material, master their instrument; they assimilate. And then the time comes when their self-referring capabilities, informed by continuous learning, brings them to the place where they are themselves; they innovate.

You can't be anybody better than you can be yourself.

DR JOHN

BACKWARD FOCUS—NOTES

Using self-referring approaches, a jazz-leader:

- works with uncertainty
- moves beyond the past
- lives, leads and follows by their own values
- is self-aware and self-reliant
- emphasises their teams' strengths
- uses situational leadership skills
- encourages others to lead
- respects followership
- learns constantly
- speaks with their own voice.

CHAPTER 2

Inward Focus:
Self<Empathy

Inward focus has the dominant influence of the self. In a positive sense this allows us to have maximum concentration on whatever we're doing, a completely one-tracked attention on ourselves. This is needed for the kind of cognitive activity that happens during solitary practice or study, for example, or while contemplating, day dreaming, or meditating.

However, if inward focus takes over, and the self has too much influence, it becomes a barrier. This will cause the individual or organisation to have a short-term, narcissistic view, to shut out external influences, and to be insensitive to others.

Inward focus causes a range of behaviours, from shyness through to egotistical brashness, all of which disrupt performance, and restrict the ability to listen and respond effectively, causing an improviser to be indecisive and timid, or grandiose and playing for applause. Just as it damages the interactions that are necessary for the flow of ideas in jazz, inward focus also damages the channels of communication in an organisation—blocking collaboration and team-work internally, while also cutting off outside influences and blinkering the organisation to change that's happening all around it.

> *As organisations become more global and the matrix environment becomes more common, their success will hinge on their leaders' ability to leverage collaborative approaches.*
> RUTH MALLOY

Jazz-leadership breaks through the barrier of inward focus by using empathic approaches, to open up communication, convey a vision with clarity, integrity and humility, expand horizons, produce deep listening, and improve collaboration.

> *It's like a message that you relate back and forth ... you want to achieve that kind of communication when you play ... it's like a conversation.*
> TOMMY FLANAGAN

WIDE VIEW

While jazz musicians have not been free from inward-focus behaviour, they've generally been less afflicted than many other groups. They've always been willing to work across cultural borders, to challenge racial bars, and to look outside of themselves in order to stimulate their imagination. They seek out different people, new collaborations, diversity, and change. Jazz itself is an open system that has continued to absorb different musical influences without losing its identity. Jazz-leaders draw inspiration from the wider milieu, are sensitive to the world around them, and have a broad field of view.

While most organisations choose to capitalise on what they already know, companies that are really creative make a concerted effort to allow thinking from the outside world to infiltrate them.

JEAN-MARIE DRU

Leaders now need to understand the changing business context far more broadly than in even the recent past—the way business is affected by current social, economic, cultural and environmental trends has to be factored into strategic decision-making. This requires having productive engagement with those outside the organisation, with open dialogue and genuine partnerships.

Empathy is the antidote to the barrier of inward focus, and part of the jazz-leader's role entails establishing an empathic environment, where everyone is heard, and where there's a mutual understanding between all the players. This is the best environment for improvisation—or innovation—through which peak performance is achieved.

There has to be a certain empathy among all the players in a group before the beauty in this music can really happen.

LEROY WILLIAMS

In order for jazz to work, the players have to develop an empathic competence, so they can hear and respond instantaneously to what is unfolding. The improvisation demands that their attention is not only focused on themselves, but on the entire group. And in the listening there has to be empathy with the other, trying to hear what's being played as clearly as possible, without being distracted, for example, by the chatter of an internal voice, technical issues, or a challenging audience. The kind of deep listening being aimed for allows space for ideas to evolve, produces the most coherent interaction with others, and is key to creative performance in any situation, group or organisation.

Interaction in a band means responding sensitively to whatever the other people are playing. It's a matter of being complementary.

RUFUS REID

LISTENING AND RESPONDING

Deep listening is a dynamic activity, with performers shifting their aural perspective continuously. When they're 'in the groove' it's possible to hear the entire soundscape, while also contributing to its shape, whether as the soloist spinning ideas, or the accompanist responding to what's being proposed— following the soloist's train of thought, nudging the vision to see where it can go, making suggestions that could take the performance somewhere else.

The goal is always to relate as fully as possible to every sound that everyone is making—but phew! It's very difficult to achieve.
LEE KONITZ

When listening is engaged and active, it conveys respect to the one who's communicating, and encourages them to continue and elaborate their perspective. When a jazz-leader listens to a player it's not to find mistakes, but to hear what's being said. This inspires the player to reach further into themselves, to give their best, to fulfil expectations, rather than to be inhibited and fearful of displeasing 'the boss.' It sets an example that the player can follow.

Play what you hear, not what you know.
MILES DAVIS

Unfortunately, new research by See shows that most business leaders don't listen well, and the more power that leaders have, the less likely they are to pay attention to what others say. They become increasingly affected by inward focus, and cut themselves off from advice and ideas, even when this would benefit themselves, and the performance of their organisation. Some exemplary organisations have leaders who make every effort to listen to what their team are saying—for example, Google actively encourages employees to pitch projects, holds regular Friday evening 'free beer' sessions where people across projects meet to share progress, and has a mailing list where ideas can be suggested or commented on.

Keep listening. Never become so self-important that you can't listen to other players.

JOHN COLTRANE

Jazz-leaders are willing to accept another's ideas, react to them in real time, and incorporate them into the collective whole, even if they don't always understand or like them. There is a constant flow of ideas to and from the musicians, which are taken, acknowledged, replied to, altered, interpreted, carried forward, or discarded—going back and forward between soloist and accompanists, provoking new directions, supporting the evolution, coalescing, and all taking place in the moment.

I rely so much on other people to give me ideas, and I take them and shape them my way and throw them back at them.

BRANFORD MARSALIS

REWARDED BY THE GROOVE

In business, the value of the individual tends to be seen in terms that promote competitiveness rather than cooperation, the concern being with individual achievement rather than their part in the progress of the whole, and tied to growth seen solely in relation to short-term profit. The most common types of reward system push people towards inward focus, causing the individual to become protective of their position and defensive about their limitations; they need to reject external influences that might threaten their position or challenge their perspective, and to be cautious about sharing an idea—in case it either brings ridicule upon them, or else dilutes their ownership of it.

However, openness is considered one of the most important elements in high-performance teams. To achieve an environment that encourages this, leaders need to shape reward systems so the short-term, individual contribution is balanced by recognition of how collaboration affects long-term objectives—to frame achievement in ways other than autonomous action, to include those who assist, who provide space, and who encourage—those who build relationships.

Collaboration outperforms competitive and individualistic behaviour. Leadership is a team effort.
JIM KOUZES

At the core of an improvising ensemble's collective intention is finding the 'groove', the place where the musical conversation is in flow; this is where the separate elements work as one, in the service of an idea in the middle, which comes to life and leads everyone, driving the action along with it.

It's natural development through common desire.
BILL EVANS

This groove—also known as being in flow, in the zone, peak performance, or forward focus—is achieved when the momentum is charged by all other components, informed by all other focuses in balance, and is moving of its own volition. This can happen for an individual in solo performance, when everything comes together in ways that are unpredictable and mysterious, when the performer is completely involved yet simultaneously standing back and watching their own performance take place. For a group to experience the

groove there must be empathy between players; the groove is found when everyone is so in sync with the common purpose that personal need is relinquished.
Paradoxically, the individual voice isn't lost—in fact, it's at its most eloquent.

> *It's that freedom of expression and expressiveness that comes through from*
> *a feeling you have of musical rapport with other people.*
>
> CARMEN LUNDY

Pete Welding, a journalist on the road with Duke Ellington's orchestra,
observed that he could hardly imagine a more disparate collection of egos
and temperaments, yet "once they come together on the bandstand there
is not a more cohesive and balanced union conceivable." Achieving this
level of communication takes years of playing together, and "from a common
understanding," for although jazz musicians can meet and play together immediately—by working within standard structures and idioms—it is extremely
rare for the level of rapport to be such that a groove can be found quickly.

> *I feel more fulfilled in this group than any I've been in. I always wanted*
> *to be part of a unit that stays together, that rehearses and builds.*
>
> HORACE SILVER

MUTUALLY EMPATHIC

To create an environment that holds the potential for this groove, the jazz-leader must choose group members whose temperaments may be at odds with each other, but who, when doing the work together, are capable of speaking as individuals while being part of the whole, of exploring and moving towards a mutual vision. Similarly, in an organisation, a jazz-leader selects judiciously, finding out what people really want to do before hiring them, then works with their specific abilities, and provides clear targets that meet the individual's personal goals while also fulfilling the organisation's objectives. Zappos, who in 2011 had 55,000 applicants for 200 jobs, has a lengthy recruitment process, starting with a series of phone-screening interviews, through to an onsite one-day visit with numerous interviews and a lunch or happy-hour outing. Even once they've been hired new recruits have a 4-week onboard training, which serves as an extended test.

It doesn't matter how qualified the candidate is; it's who fits the culture.
LYNDSEY ALLEN

The chemistry between people is not predictable, and, as Akira Tana points out, "meeting people on the bandstand is just like meeting people and interacting with them in other aspects of life." A jazz-leader learns to evaluate not only the skill and aspirations of new recruits, but also their personality, to ensure that they fit with the ethos of their organisation and with existing members. Betty Carter wouldn't listen out for a particular thing, but knew when she'd heard the right combination of chops and feeling in a prospective member. Art Blakey was very careful about due diligence when recruiting his members, finding out about "their backgrounds, and their dislikes, to bring about cohesion in the band and in the music."

Jazz is a very social music; it's a lot about your contemporaries and how everybody feeds off each other.
JOE LOVANO

Collective jazz emerges from the empathic standpoint of give and take, where musicians interpret one another's preferences, and follow each other's train of thought. This can only exist when the separate parts are mutually empathic.

Pioneering business people see business in a new light. Of course they must compete—but in nearly every case the number and variety of their competitive relationships is trifling compared to their cooperative relationships.
THOMAS PETZINGER

SOLOING AND COMPING

The soloist's part by itself is just one line in a whole painting.

BOBBY ROGOVIN

The empathy between musicians is never more necessary than when accompanying the soloist, or 'comping.' Some instruments have roles that include responsibilities of both accompanist and soloist, notably those in the rhythm section. This demands the ability to switch from making a personal statement, to supporting another's viewpoint—comping in a way that is sensitive to what is being said, rather than hearing it through the distortion of inward focus. Concentrated attention and acute empathy, as well as technical ability, are needed in order to respond instantaneously to events as they unfold. The jazz musician must be capable of switching from the role of distinctive soloist making a bold personal statement, to the subtle, supportive role of accompanist serving the needs of others.

Whenever someone plays, I play with them, and then when the next person plays I have to shift the focus, because everyone plays differently. You have to make adjustments.

TONY WILLIAMS

The accompanist follows the soloist's train of thought, and attempts to complement it, or, as Art Blakey says, "you don't overplay or get into competition with him; you make him feel good." The accompanist needs to interpret the solo, to respond and contribute, to imagine what the soloist's preference is, how much support they'd like, whether it should be a bed of sound, an intricate rhythmic pattern, occasional interjections, or nothing at all. The approach an accompanist takes will change over time, both throughout a solo, and as an arrangement progresses; subtle shading will get lost as the instrumentation becomes denser; what was appropriate at the start is unsuitable near the end.

Decisions are made in the moment, determined by the circumstances, guided by concentration and empathic competence, requiring intense listening and concentration, and working one's own presence into the complete picture. This constant, in-the-moment decision-making progress, based on others' actions, is an essential part of combined leadership/followership.

Usually everyone takes their cue from the soloist, but anyone could initiate
something and we would all follow suit ... it's a matter of give and take.
KENNY BARRON

LEADER/FOLLOWER

Jazz-leadership is inherently collaborative, social, and relational, because that's required to get the best from people living with uncertainty, people who are improvising. The improviser needs to receive empathy to be fully productive, and to provide it, for the group to be fully productive; it's reciprocal and pragmatic. In a networked economy, where partnerships are essential, this is how to be competitively effective. The collective capacity of the group is brought in not just to accomplish tasks, but to agree on and to have influence over direction; with this buy-in from everyone comes full engagement and commitment to the process.

> *Assembling a posse that can both support you and combine their expertise with yours ... these are relationships built on a deep and mutual understanding of ideas and knowledge.*
> LYNDA GRATTON

Perhaps it's because improvisation offers every individual a great deal of autonomy, the chance to have their say and to affect the direction of the music, that the idea that everyone should aspire to being a leader is not prominent in jazz. Some have found themselves reluctantly in a leadership position, yet would prefer to play a more supportive role. Bob James felt intimidated being "stuck out" in front of his band, and found it hard to feature himself on his records, "because I have so much more fun when I'm featuring other people." Not all personalities suit the role of leader and, like Bob James, enjoy and are good at complementing another's vision. They find fulfilment in accompanying and supporting others, and their status is not diminished in any way because of this preference.

Those guys didn't want to be soloists. They got their kicks out of sitting up there playing their horns and listening to the other guys playing solos.
EARL HINES

Some musicians become well-known in their role as sideman. Johnny Hodges played saxophone with Duke Ellington for over 40 years, who praised his tone as "so beautiful it sometimes brought tears to the eyes" but also described him as "never the world's most highly animated showman," which suggests—along with the longevity of his tenure—that Hodges was content with his role as sideman. Paul Desmond was Dave Brubeck's sideman for 16 years, yet seeing them on stage it would be impossible to discern the leader, and Brubeck's most famous track *Take Five* was composed by Desmond. Bill Evans considered his sidemen "responsible musicians and artists." This attitude was borne out in the way he treated them; Evans, having been clear about what was needed, gave them freedom to contribute in their own way. He knew that they'd use this space with sensitivity, and in order to benefit the total result. Because he trusted his own decision-making process, had clarity of vision, plus the ability to communicate what was needed, Evans could then let go, creating an environment where the musicians were free to express themselves, and were self-motivated to do their best work.

With Bill Evans it's a mutual exchange. Yet, in a way, it's very demanding because he lets me play so much.

EDDIE GOMEZ

Today's problems need new leaders—not the lofty dictator of before, but a leader who guides the vision of a group, the members of which take collective responsibility for performance. They are committed to the process, not because the leader is commanding them to be, but because each of them has a part to play that's aligned to their individuality, which includes a requirement that their voice is heard, an obligation to participate fully, and a say in the route that's taken. Consequently, the jazz-leader is a less parental figure than the traditional leader, and the follower is more adult. It's a more egalitarian leadership model, the kind we need when, as Tom Peters says, "no one can depend on the 'Big Corporate Fuzzball' to nurture them. Everyone is a renegade, an innovator, a leader."

Most do indeed work for an organisation. But increasingly they are not employees of the organisation. There are contractors, part-timers, temps.
PETER DRUCKER

Leadership trends show that the shift from an autocratic to a participative style is already happening, and predict that future success will depend upon the ability to be collaborative. However, how to organise this emphasis on the team without sacrificing individuality is less well recognised, yet it's crucial to the success of any leadership model; individualism is on the increase, and employees are becoming less company-centric, more mobile, and more concerned with their own personal development.

In jazz performance everyone has an opportunity to create a thing of beauty collectively, based on their own musical personalities.
MAX ROACH

In altering the traditional appearance of leader and follower, and the relation-ship between individual and team, the model of jazz-leadership also changes that of the organisation as a whole. If the orchestra is analogous to the traditional organisation, the conductor is the CEO, leading from a distance, clearly separate and at a visibly higher level than the group. On the other hand, in the jazz group, the leader and group are usually indistinguishable when viewed by the audience. The jazz leader is one of the team, active in the music, sharing the limelight when it's their turn, and standing to the side when it's another's time to lead. Even in larger ensembles, where some conducting is necessary, the jazz-leader will often guide others from an instrument, as part of the group. It's plain for everyone in the group to see that the jazz-leader is 'walking the talk,' doing exactly the same as they ask of others.

Jim Sinegal, CEO of Costco, the USA's third-largest retailer, wears a name tag that simply says "Jim," answers his own phone, and has an open office space. His personal behaviour expresses his ethos as clearly as his leadership decisions do—during the recession, no member of staff was laid off, and he refused to cut back on health benefits. Employees genuinely feel Sinegal is sincere and can see that he works as hard as they do. The result—the lowest employee turnover in the retail industry, annual revenues of $78 billion and one of the strongest consumer franchises in the world.

Sinegal is a jazz-leader, and is recognised as an anomaly. Traditional leaders are responding to the economic downturn with a swing back to command and control rather than a more democratic model. However, particularly because the downturn has coincided with a period of flux, this approach will no longer be effective. To deal with the new problems we're facing, leaders need to be equipped with different skills, particularly the soft skills—for example, inward-focus skills being discussed here, such as communication, listening, empathising and teamwork. It's likely that most traditional leaders will be resistant to this kind of change in approach, will be unable to change their mindset, and will be unwilling to enter into a power-sharing situation.

However, we need the kind of mutuality structure that jazz-leadership provides; leaders who are not afraid to be challenged or to make mistakes, who listen and learn, and who believe that valuing people rather than corralling them is the best way to achieve results.

In his music Gerry Mulligan proved that a whisper at times can be more effective and piercing than a shout.

BOB BROOKMEYER

STORIES, WORDS AND SILENCE

The language of jazz-leadership is intended to inspire, not dictate. Jazz-leaders set aside any inclination to impose their will, or to move listeners to any predetermined position—this is as impossible in improvisation as it is in a rapidly changing world. Instead, the leader carries and communicates a compelling vision, and inspires others to move that vision forward through their own special contribution, by telling their individual stories.

A key, perhaps the key, to leadership … is the effective communication

of a story.

HOWARD GARDNER

Having undertaken a rigorous learning process and consistent practice in order to prepare themselves, the improviser then uses a framework, a predetermined structure, within which to unfurl their unique tale. They learn about themselves and they share themselves in the process, telling those listening something about who they are, revealing clues about their character.

I teach musicians to look at it this way—you're in the nude; you're in

your birthday suit. People can see clean through you … you cannot hide.

ART BLAKEY

They draw their audience into the story by using motifs, themes, ideas that relate to each other, that move in time through an uncertain process. They're flexible and open to ideas from the rest of the group. They take risks. They stand in front of an audience prepared to make mistakes, ready to either turn those mistakes into the next stage of the exploration, or to let them go, moving beyond them immediately.

The first audience the leader talks to is their employees, their team, those who need to carry the vision forward. Howard Schultz, founder of Starbucks, told a story to employees about being in the "people business serving coffee," not the "coffee business serving people," giving them a sense of purpose to make a difference, and a clear ethos to be guided by. Jacqueline Novogratz founded The Acumen Fund after turning down the position of COO for Chase Manhattan Bank. Her vision—to alleviate poverty through market-orientated approaches, based on 'moral imagination.' She persuaded investors with her business acumen, with determination, and with powerful questions such as "we can send people to the Moon; we can see if there's life on Mars—why can't we get $5 [mosquito] nets to 500 million people?" The fund currently manages more the $40 million in investments.

I try to create ideas in a musical way the same as writers try to create images with words. I use the mechanics of writing in playing solos. I use quotations, commas, semi-colons.

JOE HENDERSON

Jazz-leaders don't only use sound to tell their story; they use pauses, space, and silence. They know when to be quiet and let others take charge. They don't need to impose themselves on every moment of the action, but trust others to maintain the vision, and move the process forward. Doing so gives them new ideas and renewed energy, so they're reinvigorated when they re-enter.

I always listen to what I can leave out.

MILES DAVIS

J.R.D. Tata is an example of how this leadership works in practice. His humility was legendary; he did not hesitate to give another their due, and then move to the background. He would consider others' ideas while carrying his vision, and he would give others all the responsibility he believed they could handle.

To be a leader, you have got to lead human beings with affection.

J.R.D. TATA

Clarity of message is paramount for the jazz-leader, and affects each point of the stage they set to realise their vision. They design a clear framework—such as the appropriate repertoire, arrangements and line-up. They make considered personnel choices, moving beyond the notion of satisfying a conventional job description to include relationship-based decisions, and they provide clear directions about how the group operates.

Freedom is gained through limiting your playing, disciplining yourself.

JAKE HANNA

Jazz-leaders are specific about core areas, including their strategy, but then clarity must be allowed to evolve in real time, as they share information about their intention, and others feed in their own perspectives. Having established the structure they then give ample opportunity for both individuality and collaboration.

Feedback is consistent, specific and usually immediate, occurring within the performance and made explicit through verbal and non-verbal communication. The jazz-leader can give instructions with a glance, encouragement with a nod, express frustration with a sound, and ask for support with an accent—as can anyone in the group.

The jazz-leader doesn't routinely use compliments or criticism—such opinions are largely redundant in a relationship between equals, where roles and responsibilities are clear, mistakes are transparent, and people are trusted to be doing their own work to the highest level they can, towards a common goal. As McCoy Tyner put it "I don't compare people … we bring what we have to offer."

We never discuss what solo somebody took. We never discuss our opinions because there is no opinion, there is only consensus.

ABDULLAH IBRAHIM

The Pygmalion effect—or how expectations influence behaviour—has been shown to be significant; studies show that children's IQ is raised merely by expecting them to do well, and that employees' performance improves when a manager tells them that their team has a special aptitude for a particular task. The jazz-leader understands that expectations have an enormous impact upon others' behaviour, and they are unambiguous about these—the challenge of the work contains an implied appreciation and respect for those who have been hired to undertake it. The work environment confirms these attitudes and their associated expectations. Consequently, there is less need for routine or overt complimenting, encouraging, feedback, or criticism. The jazz-leader conveys a great deal of authentic feedback without needing to say a word.

Without the calm assertiveness of the body language of leadership, the verbal language of leadership will have little, if any, effect.
STEPHEN DENNING

Some of the greatest leaders and most powerful players in jazz—including Bill Evans, John Coltrane, and Lester Young—were understated, introverted leaders. They exemplify the power of quiet among chatter, which is evident in the testimony of those who performed with them, and in the work of enduring value that they produced.

John Coltrane allowed you to develop your own inner feelings. He really allowed you the freedom to do what you wanted to do.

McCOY TYNER

Such leaders listen, and ask in-depth questions. They are calm and low-key. They speak softly and their demeanour inspires and reassures. Their standards are high, and they're as demanding of themselves as of others. This attitude, combined with deep consideration, vision, and determination, serves to convince followers of their authenticity. Because their ego isn't to the fore, they give others a great deal of freedom. In return, others strive to do their best and to reach the ideals that the leader holds themselves to.

Art Blakey is one of the greatest leaders in the world, and the reason is that he doesn't try to pretend that he knows stuff that he doesn't know.

WYNTON MARSALIS

Communication is consistently shown to be the cause of numerous difficulties in organisations. According to Peter Drucker, poor communication underlies 60 per cent of management problems; recent research shows that only 21 per cent of employees think their leader is an effective communicator, and only 9 per cent are inspired by them. Authentic leadership communicates its message in everything the leader does, rather than merely through the words they say. Bearing this in mind, it's perhaps not surprising that Jim Collins, in his book *Good to Great*, discovered that all the great companies he'd identified had "Level 5 leaders;" CEOs who displayed "personal humility" along with "professional will" headed up the companies that had outperformed all others in their industries over the long-term.

> *Eric Dolphy had a real good heart, and that alone made everyone want to do their best for him.*
> TONY WILLIAMS

The jazz-leader listens to what others say, is receptive to their ideas, and is open to taking action as a result. They prioritise all forms of communication as a route through which to create the best environment to inspire their team, and to produce peak performance. Understanding others is at the heart of effective communication, and empathy enables this kind of understanding. By using empathic approaches, the jazz-leader connects to others, inspires and empowers them, and improves all relationships to the benefit of their organisation.

> *Empathetic people are superb at recognizing and meeting the needs of clients, customers, or subordinates … they listen carefully, picking up on what people are truly concerned about, and respond on the mark.*
> DANIEL GOLEMAN

INWARD FOCUS—NOTES

Using empathic approaches, a jazz-leader:

- expands horizons
- opens up communication
- listens deeply
- rewards relationship-builders
- hires slowly
- is receptive to ideas
- guides with clarity, integrity and humility
- moves effortlessly from soloist to accompanist
- makes expectations unambiguous
- inspires through story and silence.

CHAPTER 3

DOWNWARD FOCUS: SHADOW<TRUST

D ownward focus has the dominating influence of the shadow. This is everything that goes on beneath the surface, behind closed doors, backstage. In a positive sense, the shadow encompasses our deepest experience; it's through these life events that we grow; we develop resilience and the ability to deal with the demands of human existence by meeting and rising to challenges. If these events are overwhelming then downward focus will draw attention completely, and sometimes in life that is necessary or unavoidable.

However, when the impact of downward focus is more covert, and the effect more subtly corrosive, then it becomes a barrier that sucks the spirit out of individuals and organisations, inhibiting action, draining creativity, productivity, and well-being. This barrier is at the root of workplace issues such as bullying, power play, destructive criticism, and stress. When we become aware of this barrier we have the capability to shine a light on the shadow, and remove it. But, as downward focus tends to be hidden from sight, first the issues must be revealed, otherwise downward focus will run the show, ruining an individual's potential, an organisation's purpose, and an improviser's performance.

When trust is low, in a company or in a relationship, it places a hidden 'tax' on every transaction: every communication, every interaction, every strategy, every decision is taxed, bringing speed down and sending costs up.
STEPHEN M.R. COVEY

Jazz-leadership breaks through the barrier of downward focus by using trust approaches, to recognise and remove damaging behaviour, enable risk-taking, manage mistakes, reduce stress and provide stability.

How great musicians demonstrate a mutual respect and trust on the bandstand can alter your outlook on the world and enrich every aspect of your life, understanding what it means to be a global citizen in the most modern sense.
WYNTON MARSALIS

JUDGEMENT AND CRITICISM

The general public have an idea about jazz that's not quite true.

BILL EVANS

There are some common misconceptions about jazz that have not served it well. One is that improvisation is produced through an innate 'feel,' by musicians who pluck notes out of thin air; nothing could be further from the truth. Jazz is a complex art form, born from the amalgam of African, European and African–American musical elements, and requiring disciplined study, relentless practice, and intense concentration. It's one of the world's most sophisticated musical languages, yet is poorly understood, and jazz musicians' contribution undervalued.

Unless the listener hears and studies a band seriously, there's a chance that he will form his own opinion of that organisation's ability and worth. And sometimes that's not so good.

COUNT BASIE

There have been many critics of jazz, some who loved the genre and others who loathed it, a few who were ambivalent, and many who completely misjudged it.

Some of the greatest jazz innovators have been subjected to relentless negative press. John Coltrane's early recordings were described as "musical nonsense," yet he came to be acknowledged as one of the most profound, compelling and imitated voices in jazz. Bill Evans was derided by some as little more than a cocktail pianist, while he's now recognised as a transformative master of the art form, his music exquisitely beautifully and elegantly crafted. A critic at one of Art Tatum's phenomenal performances was overheard saying, "Sure, he's great, but he fingers the keys the wrong way." When young players are thrown into the spotlight they can be bruised by the barrage of such criticism; Branford Marsalis was shocked by its intensity, not only by its viciousness, but "that the critics could actually be so inept."

Let 'em laugh, they need something to laugh at ... somebody got something to say about everything you do.
THELONIUS MONK

Being under the magnifying glass, being judged and commented upon has an impact on the performer, and consequently on the overall performance. This is rarely for the best. For Max Roach, the demand to come up with new product was relentless, and he recognised that change merely for novelty was not progress. Artie Shaw regretted that, once he became well-known, he had to satisfy those demanding new product, and no longer had time to create the "nice effects" or to prepare things properly; "they won't give you a chance to breathe." For George Benson, the outer critics went straight to his inner critic, compounding the effect on the music; "I began to worry—do people want me to sing? Some would say yes, some no. I was caught in the middle." Doubt shuts down creativity; "I became very conscious of what I was playing, whereas before, my guitar and I had always been natural ... now all of a sudden I began to pay attention to it." While self-awareness is essential to performance, self-consciousness will kill it; "we begin to examine ourselves ... there's such a thing as trying too hard."

Doubt sets in; and the musician winds up putting down the true flowering of himself and his music.

GLENN FERRIS

The external evaluation of performance is compounded by awards and polls; Wayne Shorter believes that an emphasis on external validation degrades performance and is merely a continuation of the school system; "the star you get on your paper, the ABCD mark. If we could get rid of the stigma that grading has produced, we might have a clearer idea of what a person does when he is creating something."

The pressure of external criticism, along with lack of respect or recognition for one's work or contribution, can be overwhelming for a musician, as for any employee. Fear of making mistakes inhibits creativity and performance, and fear of admitting mistakes stultifies honest dialogue, cutting off any opportunity to rectify them. When Alan Mulally, CEO of Ford Motor Company, instigated a weekly review, his employees told him that everything was fine, but the figures spoke differently. He appealed for the truth, applauding the first person who eventually dared to break it to him. So began a turnaround.

Fear of making mistakes makes people sound stiff.
RON WESTRAY

Improvisers want to perform at the highest level they can—it brings the ultimate reward of personal satisfaction. The jazz-leader understands this, and believes that criticising any lacklustre performance—particularly in front of others—is counterproductive, and will inhibit creativity and damage morale. Everyone has occasional difficulties in executing their work, and, if the jazz-leader has chosen their personnel wisely, they can allow sporadic mistakes to be dealt with by the individual themselves, with the right support mechanisms on hand if more help is needed.

Bill Frisell is a great bandleader: he provides safety for us to know we can play what we feel, and talk about it if we want to.
JOEY BARON

When one's work has personal meaning, the inner critic is a powerful voice, and as long as downward focus is in balance, this voice is a positive driving force. It guides the individual to do their best, using intrinsic motivation to spur action and to dig deeper into one's potential. However, this inner critic also has the capability to be far more pernicious and persistent than external ones. Sonny Rollins admits that he was hard on himself, and Terence Blanchard that "playing this music you're always evaluating yourself, and I guess I evaluate myself too much." When you lose confidence, "it's almost over," said trumpeter Red Rodney, and Art Farmer believed that, "it wouldn't do any good to me to have it known how I feel about my playing most of the time."

The player himself is the most severe critic of them all.
ART FARMER

Jazz musicians are not alone in having this degree of self-criticism, and walking a fine line that runs between being motivated by the inner critic and being crippled by it. Many leaders are afraid to admit their weaknesses, in case they lose credibility in a world that still appears to value a particular type of strength. However, there is a growing awareness of authentic leadership, and an understanding that, as management expert, Bill George, expresses it, "accepting your shadow side is an essential part of being authentic."

Many leaders—men in particular—fear having their weaknesses and vulnerabilities exposed. So they create distance from employees and a sense of aloofness.

BILL GEORGE

The way a leader relates to their employees has an immense impact upon which side of the self-criticism line an individual's thinking runs, and is a crucial determinant of someone's performance levels. Neuroscience, as well as our own experience, shows us that our emotional centres have a strong connection to our thinking centres; negative emotions highjack the prefrontal cortex—so when we're distressed our working memory gets used up, leaving us with less capacity to think creatively, make wise decisions, or improvise. The jazz-leader understands this, and knows that the musician's inner critic is the 'bad cop' that needs to be countered, in order to get the best from someone. Consequently, they'll encourage rather than admonish, praise rather than put down, and express trust rather than judgement. While this behaviour is kind it's also pragmatic.

He showed me by doing. He would never try to hurt my feelings and tell me what he wanted me to do.

RED RODNEY

Those who create, and particularly those who undertake the risky job of improvising in public, have to handle the constant external and internal chatter of criticism; it greets the novice and, whilst becoming tamed by experience, it never completely disappears. These same outer and inner critics greet whoever tries to be creative and innovative in any context. How they cope depends on their inner strength, their external support mechanism, the extent and nature of the criticism, as well as the broader societal and cultural environment.

Bix Beiderbecke died of a broken heart, and it was broken by the professional jealousy of musicians who couldn't stand to be outplayed by him so easily.
RED NICHOLS

Downward focus has a powerful hook in the shape of the critic, and musicians are well aware of its destructive capability; some have used this to damage other musicians. Jealousy can be behind criticism, as Red Nichols claimed was the case with Beiderbecke. The destructive critic can appear when threatened or confused by progress—Louis Armstrong said of bebop, specifically Charlie Parker and Dizzy Gillespie, "that's got nothing to do with jazz. That's Chinese music." While Roy Eldridge thought Coltrane was, "jiving! He's putting everybody on." And, because he had been classified as 'jazz,' each time Miles Davis changed direction, moved into a different style or experimented with a new technique, he was subjected to prolonged criticism from all quarters.

Musicians, driven by emotions such as competitiveness or insecurity, can be cold or critical of newcomers, alienating them by playing difficult tunes, or incredibly fast tempos, while women have historically had difficulty finding a foothold in the world of jazz, being subjected to a range of alienating downward focus behaviours, from the eroding effects of condescension, through to explicit ostracism.

There are a lot of women that play, but they've been killed off.

BARBARA DONALD

INSIDERS AND OUTSIDERS

Many organisations are wedded to the status quo and, despite policies to the contrary, tend to hire people who look like them, treating difference with suspicion. This has caused problems for many 'outsiders,' including women in jazz as well as in other workplace environments, and an enervating struggle against an undercurrent of damaging societal assumptions and prejudice. The jarring of the stereotypes of 'feminine' and 'leadership' has played a part in the prevailing imbalance of women in leadership roles. This not only hurts individual lives and wastes the collective talent pool, but it is increasingly shown to be detrimental to an organisation; companies with gender diversity at the top show an improved bottom line, such as 36 per cent better stock price growth and 46 per cent better return on equity. Add to this women's position as consumers, and the lack of women in leadership is not just a moral issue; it's foolish business. Standard Chartered realised this, and have made engaging women a business imperative and central to the bank's business strategy, as well as genuinely attempting to increase diversity within what they recognise is a generally male-dominated industry.

If a Board does not at all resemble the market being served… then something (Big) is (Badly) wrong.
TOM PETERS

Another damaging clash of stereotypes is found in 'creative people' and 'effective leaders.' A survey by IBM of 1500 CEOs showed that they now recognise creativity as the most essential leadership skill, an extraordinary shift in attitude that's primarily due to the increasing complexity of the market-place. However, the same CEOs believe that both they and their enterprises lack the requisite levels of creativity. Perhaps this can be explained in part by a bias that skews the selection process away from the creative solutions CEOs are looking for; candidates who express creative ideas are perceived as having less leadership potential, and will be passed over in favour of those who would preserve the status quo through feasible but relatively unoriginal solutions—an unconscious bias that's affecting the quality of future leadership.

Margaret Wheatley has experienced thousands of people who were responsible for excellent innovations in their organisation, who believed they would be appreciated for this, and instead "they get dismissed, pushed out of the system, or just ignored and they'll feel invisible." Talented performers, innovators, those who don't fit in with the prevailing culture, or who could be perceived as a professional threat, must be vigilant in any group or organisation. They must keep an eye out for destructive downward-focus behaviour from amongst their peers, even those whom they might expect to provide support and encouragement. The jazz-leader is alert to signs of bias, prejudice, and toxic behaviour, aware of how undercurrents affect the flow, and can destroy trust in their team.

The organization and their top management … will have to earn the trust and loyalty of the people who work for them, whether these people are their employee or not.

PETER DRUCKER

MASKS ON FRIENDS AND FOES

The jazz-leader selects people for their team who have, as Betty Carter put it, the right "chops" as well as the right "feelings;" one without the other will not work, and a negative personality drains everyone's energy and enthusiasm. The importance of trust is paramount in achieving peak performance as a group, and traits such as prejudice, jealousy, and aggression will damage morale and poison the environment. Sometimes the jazz-leader gets it wrong when choosing personnel, and it's only once the mask slips that someone's true nature is revealed. Or the musical ability of a member may prove to be insufficient in the longer term—they may not 'cut it,' being deficient in certain skills, or perhaps be stylistically unsuited. Whatever the reason, such performers have a debilitating effect on the entire performance, diverting others' energy and concentration away from the demands of improvisation. The consequence of small actions has a devastating impact on performance over a period of time.

> *The need for collaboration, inclusiveness, and building trust and relationships is becoming increasingly important as organizations continue to remove entire layers of old command and control management jobs and replace them with more matrixed leadership roles.*
>
> MARY FONTAINE

In any team, destructive behaviour from peers undermines performance, along with personal well-being. Criticism of ability can be delivered in a professional manner, yet mask a malicious intent. While personal remarks have no such cover story, they can be even more difficult to counter. These veer from the snide remark, into the realm of bullying, from Jimmy Heath's derision of another's success—saying that in New York alone he could find 20 similar players who, "with the right publicity, the right backing and the right record exposure, could be even greater,"—through to Melba Liston's hostile welcome when she arrived in New York to join Gillespie's band, and was greeted by, "why the hell did he send all the way to California for a bitch trombone player."

However, while belittling words have a profound impact, probably the most devastating effect of downward focus is when it takes hold within the performance, and support is withheld. Alienating others is an effective form of bullying, with research showing that it has a deeper psychological effect than many other forms, while being harder to identify and deal with.

There are ways in which musicians can sabotage a person's playing.
ART DAVIS

Trust throughout a group is essential for successful performance. Sometimes lack of trust can be due to the presence of an outsider, and indeed, an outside element *will* be disruptive and undermine performance if the rest of the group is entrenched in its position. The easiest solution to regain cohesion—to maintain the status quo—is to remove the outsider, and until recently this has been the default response. However, its wisdom is being challenged, not only by the outsiders who wish to participate fully, but also by jazz-leaders, who recognise it as damaging to the long-term health of their group—affecting the bottom line, curbing innovation, limiting the talent pool.

They just didn't hire me; many a time a drummer who couldn't swing half as well as I could would be hired. Those kinds of things used to hurt.
DOTTIE DODGION

If there's lack of trust in an individual—whether this is because they're perceived as an outsider, or because of their ability or personality—others will alienate them, either personally or more indirectly through the work. This undermines the individual's confidence to express themselves, to take risks or contribute fully; it means their ideas are not developed, their abilities are not stretched, and their potential is damaged. It damages their trust in themselves and in others. This process is unlikely to be explicit; rather it's an undercurrent that, over time, demoralises the individual, destroys creativity, is detrimental to the performance, and damages the organisation.

The jazz-leader is sensitive to these behaviours, and addresses them as soon as they're recognised. It's impossible to build a winning culture, one that can perform at its peak, when even one individual is a depleting influence, and such behaviour is not only destructive to performance, but also tends to be contagious and can begin a negative cycle.

When they start to play, there needs to be sincerity and truth. They're not trying to please me, but they're playing exactly who they are.
JASON MORAN

Particularly when times are uncertain, it's easy for aggressively self-serving behaviours to emerge as survival mode comes to the fore. When this happens to employees, loyalty dips and turnover rises; when it happens to a leader, it can affect the entire culture.

While Dr Laura Crawshaw's research into bullying bosses has shown that these people are often "clueless" as to the fact that they're hurting others, it makes their behaviour no easier to tolerate for the individual on the receiving end, nor less damaging to the organisation. A recent survey of 1000 employees reflects current figures that show this is a growing problem, with 69 per cent of respondents reporting workplace bullying, 44 per cent of whom claimed it was by a manager; the Advisory, Conciliation and Arbitration Service (ACAS) estimates that 18.9 million working days are lost in the UK each year as a direct result of workplace bullying.

Abusive leaders must change or quit—they will get run out of town.

JOHN HOPE BRYANT

Research from psychologist Paul Babiak indicates that as many as one in 25 business leaders is not merely a bully, but actually has psychopathic tendencies—they are "successful psychopaths." The business environment plays to their strengths, with their lack of empathy giving the impression of decisiveness, their sense of superiority conveying confidence and providing a charismatic allure, and their mask of calculated charm hiding their true intentions. Leaders with less extreme but still destructive personality traits will damage all around them. A recent study shows that a third of employees worldwide think their manager is ineffective, citing specific leadership failings such as poor listening skills, an inability to deal with conflict, favouritism, and a lack of feedback and consultation. A similar study of 60,000 workers in six countries again cites poor leadership and management behaviour as the causes of employee stress. This behaviour not only makes people ill but also causes low employee engagement and damages the bottom line—a Gallup poll estimated that in 2008 the cost of disengagement to the UK economy in the form of absenteeism, sick days and lack of productivity was between £59 billion and £65 billion. Workplace stress is on the increase, and while the economic downturn is partly to blame, it's not responsible for the whole picture.

I truly believe that this decline in the firm's moral fibre represents the single most serious threat to its long-run survival.

GREG SMITH

Greg's Smith's damning resignation letter left nobody in any doubt about his views on his former employer, Goldman Sachs, calling its environment "as toxic and destructive as I have ever seen it." Meanwhile, to the outside world, the image of the organisation was very different. Similarly, the same day that Lehman Brothers filed for bankruptcy in 2008, three top credit-rating agencies had given the company at least an A rating, meaning they were a safe investment. Flawed and unethical leadership has been the cause of many well-known corporate disasters in recent years, and no doubt many less well-publicised ones as well. Leadership that's corrupted by downward focus hides behind stellar corporate histories and standard ways of doing business that ignore the human element.

Human behaviour is as hard as it gets; it is a lot harder than accounting figures that bear only rear view mirror witness and well tested ways of accounting for material costs

MICHAEL REDDY

While downward focus hides behind the mask of respectability and charisma, it can be spotted in cliques, scathing personal remarks, bullying, ostracism, and in the confusion and stress it spreads around. The jazz-leader is alert to the tell-tale signs, and is quick to swoop on them, recognising them for what they are, investigating the reasons for it, and rooting them out. These behaviours need to be eliminated, in order to regain the level of trust that's essential for peak performance.

Old management and leadership styles, based on a convention of low-trust/high control sit uneasily against a paradigm of 'volunteer' knowledge workers, who are expected to be accountable and empowered, willing and able to create shared learning and intellectual capital.

GARY HAMEL

Currently, only 49 per cent of employees trust senior management, and only 28 per cent believe that CEOs are a credible source of information. Trust has to start at the top. Another kind of lens is needed—one that identifies human flaws—for downward focus to be revealed. Until then, the same gloss will continue to be applied.

Trust cannot become a performance multiplier unless the leader is prepared to go first.

CRAIG WEATHERUP

TRANSFORMING MISTAKES

Mistakes are an essential part of invention, experimentation, creativity, and innovation, yet they are feared, frowned upon, avoided, denied, and very rarely rewarded by organisations. The jazz performer has to come to terms with making mistakes, and making them publically. The act of improvisation entails error; it's a given that you will make mistakes. In fact, Coleman Hawkins believed that "if you don't make mistakes you aren't really trying." Not only are mistakes inevitable in improvisation, but so is the likelihood of mediocrity, an 'off' night, and looking foolish. All this takes place in front of others, so it's possible for everyone to hear the errors and to see who has made them—they can't be covered up or the blame shifted. And others, as we've seen, can be extremely critical and unforgiving, to say nothing of the ever-demanding inner critic. Yet jazz makes this work.

In jazz there are no mistakes, only opportunities ... the mistakes are sometimes the only part that's jazz.

JON HENDRICKS

Mistakes are integral to innovation. Bill Gates has always viewed them as valuable learning lessons, and believes that "your most unhappy customers are your greatest source of learning." At Google, Eric Schmidt works on the premise of "please fail very quickly so that you can try again." While Larry Page believes that if employees don't make any mistakes, they're not taking enough risk.

No one likes to make mistakes, but the jazz-leader understands that mistakes are inevitable. Those made due to lack of ability are not tolerated for long, by peers certainly, but primarily by the player themselves—usually it will impel them towards immediate practice to address the deficiency. However, errors made as part of the exploration process are expected and accepted; it's what you do with them that matters.

It was when I found out I could make mistakes that I knew I was onto something.

ORNETTE COLEMAN

Joe Sample defines a sustaining attitude that jazz musicians have to mistakes, when he acknowledged that he played many wrong notes, "but I know it will sound like a masterpiece based upon what I do immediately after."

Sometimes the error will be something nobody else notices—it merely jarred with the musician's intention and therefore sounded wrong to their ear. When George Benson realised that these errors were not being picked up on by others because "they didn't know what I meant to play" he became liberated; "once I found that out, I was gone!"

During a performance a musician can lose track of the structure, or perhaps the beat has been turned around and they've not followed it, or their ideas become muddled—whatever the reason, experimentation entails the risk that they might lose their place or their thread of thought.

Sometimes, while playing, I discover two ideas, and instead of working on one, I work on two simultaneously and lose the continuity.

JOHN COLTRANE

However, musical errors go together with musical 'saves' in jazz, where musicians use musical, visual or verbal cues to get the music back on track. These are tactical and tactful responses made by others in the group, to support, clarify and resolve the situation. The mistakes may be forgotten immediately, or they may create a tension that's used productively, that's built on, taking the group away from the expected and into something new. This support from a team makes it possible to experiment, trusting that ideas can be tried out, and that errors are an accepted element of the process.

When you remove the fear of failure, impossible things suddenly become possible.

REGINA DUGAN

During performance there is a constant flow of appraisal, feedback and adjustment; the musicians will do this of themselves and each other, and will respond to the feedback they get from their audience. If any mistakes happen or issues arise that aren't dealt with satisfactorily during the performance, they will be addressed afterwards—the post mortem is a time to review such matters, to raise problems, iron out uncertainties, or make suggestions based upon the experience of the performance. The jazz-leader's feedback happens quickly, is about specific issues, and is concerned with solutions rather than blame.

When Toyota recalled 2.3 million vehicles for faulty brakes there was a public outcry. Instead of dealing with this mistake through a glossy PR campaign, President and COO of Toyota USA, Jim Lentz, went to the web, and entered into a dialogue on Digg. It was a transparent interview, with some 1000 questions submitted and voted on. Not only did it increase the public's trust in Toyota, but with Lentz's subsequent promotion to a post never previously held by an American, it appears to have also increased Toyota's trust in Lentz.

Engaging in candid conversation means that people are held accountable for their results, and trust can be (re)built. Nobody needs to be humiliated or punished unnecessarily in the process, with shame only serving to bring down the shutters on creativity, and stultify future performance.

Jazz is like a great void; it waits patiently until a brave musician takes control of space and time.

CHRIS GRIFFIN

Jazz-leaders need courage. It takes bravery to leap into the unknown, rather than to play stock phrases within your comfort zone or do something you know guarantees applause. But this bravery opens up new ways of doing things, taking the musician down roads that they may not otherwise have considered, and is "an incredible learning experience," observes Fred Hersch. Consequently, mistakes become a trigger for the imagination, suggesting a new motif that can become a feature, inspiring the development of a solo, being absorbed into the flow. The mistake is transformed, while being itself the transformer, a catalyst for change.

That's how jazz was born. Somebody goofed. You stop doing that and start getting clinical, you don't play jazz any more.

ART BLAKEY

TRUSTING SELF AND OTHERS

Improvisers learn to get beyond the noise of outer and inner critics; they need to dampen down the voices of doubt, to be brave and keep moving. To achieve this, they have to trust themselves. McCoy Tyner is now less interested in analysing how he plays, seeing part of maturity as being happy with yourself, regardless of what anybody is saying about you. Improvisers have to contend with the fluctuations of popularity, with friendships that change "simply because you are now going places that you didn't go before," says George Benson, which includes the changes of musical direction that others tend to criticise. Trusting that these moves are right for both oneself and one's group, despite the doubters, involves experience and getting to know and accept oneself. It is beyond confidence, and into the realm of personal accountability and authenticity.

I used to be very hard on myself. I'm grateful for those moments of non-judgemental attitudes toward my playing. I'm enjoying myself a lot more.
MICHAEL BRECKER

Musicians performing together need to trust one another on many levels—to be sure of others' musical capabilities, to know they can count on others' support, and to believe in others' commitment to and understanding of the overall vision. They also need to trust their own contribution to the group, to believe they are doing what is required, and more, that they're making a difference. "Play it with authority, like you mean to play it. You can't make me believe it if you don't believe it," was the advice Jack McDuff gave George Benson, who adds, "I've been doing it that way ever since." Musicians may not always understand one another's approach, but they will, for example, suspend judgement and trust the soloist, following where the solo takes them, and putting themselves fully into that train of thought.

Playing together every night, you begin to know each other, trust each other. The band begins to come together. Otherwise it just can't make it.
ART BLAKEY

The trust that Art Blakey talks of is the essential ingredient for 'groove,' the shared feel, the interplay that gives the music a life of its own, allowing it to become the 'the idea in the middle' of its component parts. This is the state that enables risk-taking, hushes the chatter of doubt and judgement, promises total engagement and unqualified support, and allows every performer to be both leader and follower.

Employees working at Innocent, the number one smoothie brand in the UK, talk about the reasons they love working there—"I can be myself," "no two days are the same;" "it pushes me to be the best that I can;" "we get loads of opportunities to grow in our role;" "I get to work with my friends." The company has grown from a team of 3 people to 250 in its 12 years. It's very clear about the kind of people it recruits—those who are natural, entrepreneurial, have transferable skills, are commercially astute, have passion, and are self-leaders, in addition to which they need to understand the mission and believe in the values of the company. So work is personal. And Innocent's informal, supportive and fun environment brings out the best in people, creating an authentic culture of trust.

It was difficult to have to relinquish control. But I understood that in order for my employees, and thus myself, to be successful I needed to learn to develop a cohesive and collaborative team, beginning with trust as the framework.

JILL CLEVELEND

The freedom of improvisation needs the stability of trust. It's impossible to be creative if your confidence is eroded by criticism, if you question each move you make, if you're toppled by every mistake that occurs. Innovation will not emerge if people are undermining each other, if they're unwilling to explore new ideas, are threatened by diversity and difference, or are afraid of looking foolish.

Jazz-leaders understand this, and build a culture of trust. They pay attention to what is happening, to the environment, the relationships. They provide clear structures and genuine support, enabling people to take risks, explore new possibilities, and to be self-expressive while working with others on a combined task. They see mistakes as part of the process and an opportunity to learn and improve. The culture of trust encourages individuality to be expressed, within a group united in a groove, from which peak performance and innovation emerges.

All companies need to think again about what they do to build trust, and to think again about how they make, give, and add value.

INDRA NOOYI

DOWNWARD FOCUS—NOTES

Using trust approaches, a jazz-leader:

- praises, encourages, supports

- stays alert to toxic behaviours, and removes them

- is authentic

- has courage

- welcomes outsiders, diversity, difference

- manages and makes use of mistakes

- dampens the critical voice and dulls the fear of failure

- gives feedback quickly and specifically

- enables risk-taking

- provides stability.

CHAPTER 4

LEFT FOCUS:
LOGIC<INTUITION

Left focus has the dominant influence of logic. In a positive sense, logic is necessary and desirable, providing reasoned argument, objective decisions and practical responses, along with vital structures, systems and processes.

However, the linear, mechanistic thinking epitomised by left-focus thinking, first codified for organisations by Taylor's scientific management movement, is still the major influence in business one hundred years after Taylor's death. This approach has spread throughout everything in our lives, affecting our values, our education system, our attitudes to work, and our understanding of progress, growth, and success. Its pre-eminence is increasingly understood to be a crippling barrier in our changing world.

Data is only available about the past, and when we teach people that they should be data driven and fact based and analytical as they look into the future we condemn them to take action when the game is over.

CLAY CHRISTENSEN

Jazz-leadership breaks through the barrier of left focus by using intuitive approaches, to balance analysis with imagination, to improve engagement through purposeful work, to value process, to raise performance by working in harmony with human motivation, to use creative provocations, to loosen control, inspire and improvise.

An idealistic vision is what motivates all of us. We want to know that we are working toward something consequential, something noble. This simple truth applies to every single person within your organization, from the receptionists to the general managers.

DOUGLAS R. CONANT

SYSTEM MELTDOWN

What underlies the current malaise in so many larger organisations worldwide is that their theory of business no longer works.

PETER DRUCKER

Even when things are going well, change is hard to make. The success trap has claimed a slew of famous victims—not only individuals, or companies, but entire industries, whose leaders did not respond effectively to change. Barnes and Noble, the USA's largest bookstore chain, was one of the first to enter the realm of digital books—but it didn't stay the course, exiting its investment in an e-reader too early, and re-entering when Amazon's Kindle had already cornered the market. Their downfall, like many others, wasn't due to a lack of resources or ability, but due to left-focus logic persuading them to stay with what they knew, regardless of whether it was still pertinent. To left focus, the existing way of doing things is comprehensible—this trumps the fact that it's no longer relevant.

Leaders must encourage their organizations to dance to forms of music yet to be heard
WARREN BENNIS

In the midst of uncertainty, the logic of left focus kicks in even more insistently. When individuals, and therefore organisations, are under stress, the default behaviour is to go with what's familiar, to hunker down, take no risks, stay with the known, and conserve energy. This strategy is not only more likely in times of transition and upheaval, but it's also more dangerous, particularly now, given the global consequences of mismanagement. While it's as incongruous, and as bound for failure as an improviser regurgitating stock phrases, leaders have been guided by left-focus logic for so long that it's hard for them to extract themselves from its paradigm, and not only envisage another way of being but do the necessary work to become it.

Most leaders are the victim of the freedom not to struggle. You have to be completely merciless with yourself.

KEITH JARRETT

The command and control of left focus lurks just below the surface of much talk concerning change and innovation. Margaret Wheatley's work demonstrates that innovative individuals in organisations "rarely, very rarely get brought into decisions, or are told that they really have something to teach." Large systems are resistant to innovation, and "they still seek to push it aside, ignore it, and, in many cases, push the person out as well." Left focus believes that it's best for a system to control people rather than vice versa, because a system can be built on specific processes with clear functions—this is easy for left focus to understand; on the other hand, it finds human behaviour intolerably muddling. Left focus thinks people should change to suit the system, and consequently most organisations still design systems from this premise. The overriding consideration in all systems derives from short-term, quantifiable results and how these impact the bottom line. The effect of the system on the human beings who operate within it is generally ill-considered and of secondary importance, producing environments that are stultifying.

Show me a company that loses all the time and I'll show you bad morale.

JAMIE DIMON

At Southwest Airlines they follow the maxim of "employees first, customers second, shareholders third." This prioritisation is intended to ensure that employees feel good about what they're doing, have a sense of belonging to the company, and then, as Colleen Barrier, Southwest's President Emeritus explains, in exchange will "do the same thing by offering our passengers the same kind of warmth, caring, and fun spirit." This is the way of jazz-leadership; leaders take care of their people, who then take care of the customer—the audience—creating a loyal fan base, producing results which satisfy shareholders.

It's not just for CEOs and managers, it's for all of us—lead with love, appreciate people and they'll come alive and you'll get great results.

KEN BLANCHARD

A bureaucratic, left-focus organisation, of whatever size, has no place for the individual, and only gives employee well-being perfunctory consideration, where it obviously impacts the immediate bottom line. Because of this disconnect, employees in left-focus organisations feel a sense of powerlessness—which may explain in part why over 50 per cent of the UK workforce is estimated to spend 50 per cent of their time looking for a new job, in the hope of finding more personal satisfaction and self-expression; in the USA, a recent Gallup poll estimated that the cost of employee disengagement was equivalent to 35 per cent of payroll.

Is it possible for business leaders to realise that the dilemmas they are facing cannot be solved by their traditional management behaviour, their traditional management tools?
MARGARET WHEATLEY

MOTIVATION, GOALS AND REWARDS

The reward for playing jazz is playing jazz.
JOHN LEWIS

Standard reward systems are built on the belief that humans are motivated primarily by financial incentives. However, along with real-world examples of ventures built by volunteers, such as Wikipedia and Open Source technology, there is a growing body of research that contradicts this assumption. In fact, Daniel Pink's work cites research—undertaken by economists, funded by the

Federal Reserve Bank—that proves what many studies have shown before: when work requires even rudimentary cognitive skills, a larger financial reward leads to poorer performance. Once people are paid enough to remove money as an issue—and this is less than might be imagined—there are three factors that lead to better performance: autonomy, mastery and purpose. Jazz-leadership has all three of these motivators at its core, and by tapping into them it achieves an engaged, highly skilled workforce, whose continuously improving performance fulfils the individual's personal needs while benefiting the organisation.

The recently launched Metro Bank is doing the business of banking in a new way, based on convenience and good service. They deliver the latter by taking great care in the recruitment process—interviewing 3500 people for the first 60 customer-facing roles—and then training employees to provide excellent service and rewarding them for this, rather than for hitting sales targets.

What do you get if you motivate people to sell things? More than 11,000 complaints about UK banks every day. What happens if you reward people for giving great service? For us it's 94% customer satisfaction rate.
ANTHONY THOMSON

Supporting this approach is research from Amabile and Kramer, which shows that making progress in meaningful work produces better performance from people than material motivators, yet managers are unaware of this. Contrary to left-focus principles, typical reward systems are not only counterproductive, but may also induce self-centred risk-taking that damages the company.

When the profit motive becomes unmoored from the purpose motive, bad things happen.

DAN PINK

Similarly, the accepted practice of goal setting to motivate employees has been shown to have harmful side-effects, such as degrading performance, shifting focus away from important but non-specified goals, and damaging interpersonal relationships. Goal setting clarifies our aims, but if the goals are too narrow and prescriptive they will literally blind us to possibilities, stifle experimentation, and cause us to overlook other important features of the task. In addition, given the left-focus orientation of most organisations, goal setting is likely to ignore qualitative improvements, as these don't produce the kind of data that fully satisfy accepted management models.

Most organisations don't have a clue how to manage 'stretch goals'.

STEVE KERR

Lopsided recognition of achievement, misunderstanding of human behaviour, and paucity of imagination makes most motivation-and-reward systems not merely ineffective, but counterproductive—reducing intrinsic motivation, distorting risk preferences, and increasing unethical behaviour. This is further compounded if the wrong goal is set, such as stipulating revenue rather than profits.

Enron executives were meeting their goals, but they were the wrong goals.
SOLANGE CHARAS

The paradigm unravels even further when used in rapidly changing circumstances; how rational is it to define specific goals while heading into an uncertain future? If a leader works to a fixed script, it's likely that attention will be given to something of diminishing relevance, which employees will strive to manifest, manipulating events purely to reach their personal targets and satisfy their superiors.

Organisations tend to set employees narrow but ambitious goals and punish failure, while rewarding executives whether or not performance is weak. This increases employee stress and resentment, while producing a culture of lying and cheating, and incentivising massive risk-taking. There are numerous recent examples of how this approach damages individuals, organisations and society, particularly, but not solely, in the financial services sector, yet it is still entrenched within current business models.

Our theories about the fundamental goal of corporations and the optimal structure of executive compensation are fatally flawed ... acting on these theories, we have built structures into our capital markets system that threaten the future of American capitalism.

ROGER MARTIN

If the jazz performer was rewarded solely on the basis of an external evaluation, with predetermined performance metrics and the expectation of a 'perfect' outcome, they would fail every time; improvisation would be impossible and the performer would lose interest. If an organisation takes this stance and only rewards outcomes, rather than process, then innovation, too, is virtually impossible.

Managers and investors alike must understand that accounting numbers are the beginning, not the end, of business valuation.

WARREN BUFFET

Jazz-leaders believe that evaluation should be on process, effort and commitment to the project, and on the way mistakes are transformed, turned into points of departure, and learned from. Rewards based on how much value is added to an organisation can occur even when an outcome isn't successful. This produces what Stanford University psychologist, Carol Dweck, calls a "growth mind-set." When the jazz-leader prizes process, and rewards the 'value-added' rather than merely the outcome, it gives the individual an unambiguous message that reasonable risk-taking is expected, and passion, dedication, growth and learning are valued. All new hires at Apple receive a note which is clear in its message: "people don't come here to play it safe. They come here to swim in the deep end." Simple gestures make a huge difference. Sending hand- written notes to employees deserving of recognition is a method used by CEOs such as Alan Mullally at Ford and Jim Pack at AdvanceMD, while Calgon have an award for "the best idea that didn't work," as a way of rewarding creativity and risk-taking, and stimulating innovation. Showing appreciation and recognising employees' contribution to the process has a profound impact on morale and productivity.

Nothing is ever fully realized, and you never say "well, this is it." You're always on your way somewhere. Playing is generally a never-ending state of getting there.

ART FARMER

All improvisers, including jazz-leaders, set their own goals, based on process, away from the performance arena. During practice, every musician makes their own specific improvement plans, and monitors not only their actions, but also their own thinking about those actions; metacognition enables them to understand the problems they need to resolve. During performance, this same process-based self-observation carries on, with continuous feedback from themselves, the group, the audience, and the music itself. After performance they will reflect on what happened, judging themselves against standards they've set themselves, and building further practice upon these observations. Post mortems with others rarely discuss personal performance issues, but rather matters that affect the group as a whole, such as alterations to arrangements or repertoire.

Life at most companies seems ingeniously designed to defeat all the principles of deliberate practice: it isn't designed to make us better at anything (meet goals—get on with it).

GEOFF COLVIN

Deliberate practice is the individual's responsibility; they are in the best position to determine what needs improvement and how to achieve it, occasionally seeking external support, such as lessons from a teacher, or the opinion of a respected peer. But this is self-motivated, and consequently the individual accepts how long each step will take, has ownership of the undertaking, and understands that this demanding process will be ongoing.

If you understand the problem then you can enjoy your whole trip through.

BILL EVANS

The process, evaluation and reward systems favoured by jazz-leaders set up conditions that engage the individual, so they pick up problems as they happen, take calculated risks, are courageous, support one another, learn and relearn. They have ongoing inner dialogue, and are alert to the moment, ready to adjust their approach in response. Having been more tuned in *during* the process, once the process is complete, they are better equipped to communicate the learning that's been gleaned from it, and adapt their own behaviour and the group's overall strategy. This approach can be applied to anyone, in any role, in any organisation—producing the autonomy, mastery and purpose that improve performance.

The only way to build a company that's fit for the future is to build one that's fit for human beings as well ... to build a 21st century management model that truly elicits, honors, and cherishes human initiative, creativity, and passion—these tender, essential ingredients for business success in this new millennium.

GARY HAMEL

JAZZ PROVOCATIONS AND CONFLICT

Jazz-leaders recognise that human behaviour is such that we need and want nudges to consistently refocus us on our endeavours, to keep us alert when familiarity or lazy thinking could dull our creativity, to keep us growing when inertia would be an easier short-term option. But they don't motivate their team by linking performance to targets, benchmarks or goals. Instead they set up the environment for peak performance—and then they create small disruptions that tease themselves and others out of complacency. To shake up clichés and inspire innovation, jazz-leaders consistently cultivate provocative competence. They are skilled at devising provocations that aren't toxic or controlling, but rather a means by which to keep the senses sharp, an invitation to themselves and others to keep exploring.

Joe Henderson inspires me to always reach the depths of every tune.
RENEE ROSNES

The jazz-leader's provocations take a variety of forms. One is through the design of the group, the line-up—the instrumentation and musical personalities. Miles Davis would repeatedly disband his groups and form new ones, and when Max Roach changed his personnel around, he'd intentionally look for people who didn't sound like those they were replacing. Duke Ellington actively sought out and celebrated difference in the musicians he hired, believing this fuelled creativity, bringing about "playing within context," a phrase used by McCoy Tyner to describe how he's inspired to perform in different ways by the musical personalities he surrounds himself with. Tim Smit, CEO of the Eden project, takes similar action by regularly moving employees out of role, so that rather than getting stuck into a routine they keep their energy, and that of the company, flowing.

> *I like to work in as many different musical environments as possible and to be given the chance to express myself within each one.*
> EDDIE GOMEZ

Jazz is inherently composed of diverse teams, and improvisers seek out different environments to develop their musical voice—so team turnover works for everyone; it's a normal part of the creative process, and it's in the nature of the art form to seek inspiration through change. Some jazz groups stay together for many years, performing regularly, evolving tunes through repeated playing, and becoming familiar with each other's musical mannerisms. They will use provocations other than team turnover to maintain the creative energy, injecting them into the music itself—altering arrangements, swapping solos around, shifting time or feel, playing in obscure keys, and so on.

As a group, we get a chance to evolve the music. You have to play tunes over and over in different settings on different occasions.

HERBIE HANCOCK

Many groups are fluid units, eliminating the possibility of people becoming stale, burnt-out or bored, of outgrowing their position; this brings new knowledge and perspectives into the group, creating original combinations, allowing fresh interplay between old and new ideas.

At DaVita they use job rotation to give their leaders an in-depth, hands-on understanding of the demands faced by employees at the frontline of their business; Steve Priest, DaVita's chief wisdom officer and senior vice president of operations, believes that "developing human beings' emotional intelligence and self-awareness is critical to great leadership and great teams."

Research by Brian Uzzi on groups concluded that the best teams were, by far, "those with a mix of relationships ... these teams had some old friends, but they also had newbies." Shaking up a team so there's a mix of relation-ships keeps energy and ideas flowing, and Uzzi's extensive study shows this makes for financial success.

This mixture meant that the members could interact efficiently—they had a familiar structure to fall back on, but they also managed to incorporate some new ideas. They were comfortable with each other, but they weren't too comfortable.

BRIAN UZZI

Proctor and Gamble are recognised as an innovative culture, and innovation seen as the cornerstone to their success. They have set up numerous methods through which to achieve it, including a research and development organisation of over 8000 employees, a dedicated innovation team, and innovation centres which simulate in-home and in-store environments. They challenge their people, from day one, through hands-on experience.

Skype's goal is to be disruptive in the cause of making the world a better place.

NIKLAS ZENNSTRÖM

Not rehearsing as a group is another form of provocation used by the jazz-leader. For anything beyond working within rudimentary forms, this demands a great deal from the improvisers, making for intense concentration and spontaneity when they come together in performance. Miles Davis would tell his musicians, "I pay you to practice on the bandstand," and he used this approach in concerts and in the studio. His classic 1959 recording *Kind of Blue* provides a definitive exemplary example of work produced from this stance. Davis presented musicians with sketches, unfamiliar forms, unusual scales and chords; he offered them no rehearsal before recording all tracks, mostly done in a single take. By doing this, Davis provoked the musicians beyond their familiar thought-processes, and created what is still recognised as one of the most evocative and imaginative jazz explorations. His disruption was challenging, but it was affirmative—a mark of respect for and trust in his musicians' capabilities. The outcome was unknown when they began; the targets that Davis provided for the team were just enough to give them a framework within which to work, while giving them the responsibility and allowing them the freedom to use their skills to the full, for the benefit of the collective work. There was no other incentive needed for these individuals to devote themselves to achieving peak performance.

The jazz-leader creates a stable environment which can withstand disruptive provocations designed to encourage new ways of thinking and to improve the quality of the improvisation.

You know why I don't play any ballads anymore? Because I like to play ballads so much

MILES DAVIS

Choosing diverse individuals to work as a team, choosing to lose valuable skills and knowledge on a regular basis, choosing to go to the bother of frequently working in new hires, as well as the willingness to train up new leaders who will move on and become competitors—these would traditionally be viewed as undesirable, unsettling and negative, rather than being strategies of choice, as they are for the jazz-leader. Indeed, conflict does arise from these approaches, which a jazz-leader must manage, maintaining harmony in the group despite uncertainty being the normality. They are not afraid of removing personnel if too much conflict permeates the organisation—they are slow to hire and quick to fire; they will change instrumentation if circumstances call for it; they may disband entirely. However, integral to the jazz-leadership approach is the ability to reach consensus while dealing with multiple constituencies. And not only is the problem of conflict outweighed by the value that disruptive strategies bring, but conflict itself is inextricably linked to the creative process, and is therefore, to a degree, expected and accepted by everyone.

Very few people are good in dealing with conflict. Conflict, when dealt with appropriately, could be very generative but many people end up just having fights in the name of conflict management. They don't really harness the creative potential.

PETER SENGE

IMPROVISATION

You have to choose to be secure like a stone, or insecure but able to flow.

KEITH JARRETT

The 'Kind of Blue' approach—and improvisation more broadly—can give a false impression of random spontaneity, which is partly why jazz is poorly understood. In reality, the jazz musician must first have technical fluency on their instrument, then understand the complex language and absorb the work of established players, and finally transcend imitation and develop their own sound. It takes extensive time and study to reach the point where the logic and routine of left focus can be moved beyond, where it's no longer in control but is in the service of voicing new thoughts, of improvising.

It's taken me 20 years of hard work and playing experience to do as well with it as I can. There is no shortcut.

BILL EVANS

Improvisation is "the product of all that players have experienced, all the music they've studied, absorbed, deleted and refined" according to Walter Bishop Jnr. It's evolutionary and involves the intellectual and the intuitive, "learning from within and from without." This process of action based on intuition, informed and supported by learning but not driven by it, is one of jazz-leadership's key characteristics.

Modern intelligence means intuition.
PHILIPPE STARCK

Because organisations are under pressure to perform in ways that satisfy left-focus thinking, most leaders dare not undermine left focus and allow their intuition to steer. It is as Einstein noted, "the intuitive mind is a sacred gift and the rational mind is a faithful servant. We have created a society that honors the servant and has forgotten the gift." To dislodge this accepted way of working from its preeminent role invites criticism, especially if things go wrong; only the most courageous leaders dare to shake up the status quo to such an extent.

The cultures that grow from left focus would never approve the Kind of Blue approach, as they need to pin down the expectations, map out the process, and know the outcome before the journey has begun. They have yet to accept how much improvisation and retrospective sense-making are now required in business, how often leaders have to act without a clear understanding of the way things will unfold. Leaders are already improvising, they have no choice. But most are doing it using an outdated language; they have yet to learn the syntax of improvisation.

Intuition is a very powerful thing—more powerful than intellect.

STEVE JOBS

When a leader is under scrutiny and any mistakes would be made in the public eye, they're most likely to stick to the well-trodden path. But this is not the way of the improviser, or the jazz-leader, and it's not the way new solutions will be found to new problems. Rather, leaders have to be genuinely brave. They have to reduce their level of control, design environments that allow people to be self-actualising while also committed to a common vision, and learn the syntax of jazz-leadership so they can communicate in the language of change—so they can improvise.

Improvising is difficult. It's like life.

JANICE ROBINSON

CONTROL AND SURRENDER

For left-focus leaders, the priority is to maintain order and control, and, when hit by times of uncertainty such as an economic downturn, they are likely to put so much emphasis on cost-cutting and bottom-line efficiency that their greatest assets—people—are pushed to one side. Employees, particularly top performers, are rebelling against this behaviour; they feel undermined, ignored or taken for granted. Large companies, including Yahoo, General Electric and Home Depot, report having problems keeping their best people, who are disenchanted with bureaucracy, with managers who never express appreciation or show interest in employees' career progression, with a lack of stimulating work or a vision they can get behind, and with poor leadership. Their complaints are less about income, more about a dearth of opportunity and development. The message is beginning to get through—in 2011, 'people issues' didn't even figure in the KPMG Business Leaders Survey of 3000 leaders in Europe and the Middle East; in 2012 it was ranked in fifth place, and it was deemed crucial to offer development opportunities to key people.

You cannot expect to perform at a high level unless people are personally engaged. It's foundational for a high-performing company.
DOUG CONANT

Still, leaders appear unaware that their behaviour is at the root of employees' lack of engagement, seemingly complacent about their own leadership capabilities and seeing no need to reconsider their approach or to upskill themselves. Recent research from the Chartered Institute of Personnel and Development found that 72 per cent of employers believe there is a deficit of leadership and management skills; a key problem in tackling this is that managers don't recognise their failings—there's a gaping 'reality gap' between managers' self-perception and the views of their employees. In some cases, managers are promoted because they have good technical skills, but they receive inadequate leadership training. Nevertheless, even leaders who have received training in business schools are not guaranteed to have the skills necessary for today's world. Author and business academic, Henry Mintzberg; Rakesh Khurana from Harvard Business School; Jeffrey Pfeffer from Stanford; Scott McNealy, co-founder of Sun Micro-systems, are among those who have been vociferous in their criticism of management education and the type of executives and leaders it produces.

We—as business school faculty—need to own up to our own role in creating Enrons. Our theories and ideas have done much to strengthen the management practices that we are all now so loudly condemning.

SUMANTRA GHOSHAL

Business schools have responded to the criticisms, and recognise that the requirements of leadership are changing. The approach taken in MBA programmes is being broadened, enabling participants to develop academic, employability, and soft skills. This is not only for the benefit of students, but also for the business schools, with the inclusion of leadership and soft skills deemed necessary to keep the MBA in demand. Whether these changes will bring about the kind of jazz-leadership that's now required is as yet unknown. But what is more certain is that leaders—or future leaders—need to overcome the imbalance that's caused by the prevalent left-focus bias.

We need fewer techies and more poets in our systems design shop. And more artists…and more jazz musicians…and more dancers…period. (Or, rather, consider that an action item).

TOM PETERS

Just as organisational innovation is destroyed when command and control takes the helm, so an improviser will hit the barrier of left focus if they attempt to self-consciously over-think their performance, rather than allowing their intuitive responses to come to the fore, supported by their logical side. This can happen for a variety of reasons: some musicians lose confidence in their instinctive direction, particularly if it's innovative; some vacillate when confronted by differing critical reactions to their work and attempt to satisfy others by distorting their natural musical inclinations; some get caught in the success trap—the improviser who has reached a mass audience can find themselves at risk of losing their creative edge.

You sacrifice a certain amount of fresh searching and probing to give people

what they want to hear.

EDDIE GOMEZ

If the improviser over-thinks the process, the performance will become stilted. If the jazz-leader *strives* to attain the state that allows 'groove' they will only block it—like squeezing water, it drains away. Instead, they must surrender familiar control processes, and draw on their accumulated knowledge, ideas and thoughts, allowing the expression of that wisdom to emerge, without cognitive processes attempting to rationalise or judge it.

In the business community, the accepted leadership approach functions within the familiar confines of left focus. But for the jazz-leader, this modus operandi is unsatisfactory, incompatible with the level of innovation that they're aiming for. Rather than controlling the action, left focus needs to provide the frame within which freedom, unpredictability, and improvisation take place. Traditionally contemptuous of competencies such as collaboration, flexibility, empathy and collective leadership, left-focus logic must now make way for them, and take a supporting role.

Part of what made the Macintosh great was that the people working on

it were musicians and poets and artists and zoologists and historians who

also happened to be the best computer scientists in the world.

STEVE JOBS

LEFT FOCUS—NOTES

Using intuitive approaches, a jazz-leader:

- takes care of their team
- taps into the desire for autonomy, mastery, and purpose
- values process, effort, initiative, commitment and passion
- nudges with creative provocations, and expects conflict
- rewards in harmony with human motivation
- shows appreciation little and often
- uses their intuition
- balances analysis with imagination
- understands the syntax of improvisation
- surrenders familiar control processes.

CHAPTER 5

Right Focus:

Imagination<Structure

R ight focus has the dominant influence of imagination, the positive aspects of which are perhaps self-evident, particularly in a time of rapid change where creativity and innovation are the vital survival tools. As we've seen, focuses become barriers when their dominant influence draws too much attention, pulling individual or organisational behaviour out of balance. However, right focus is a somewhat different case, when it comes to organisations; while some companies will flounder because a concentration on imagination causes a lack of structure, in general the barrier of right focus in organisations is due to *lack* of attention, rather than over-emphasis.

Business hasn't paid much attention to right focus, viewing its abstract, non-linear, qualitative characteristics with disinterest, even contempt—these particularly human qualities have been seen as weaknesses, as liabilities to be discouraged rather than assets to be developed. In many organisations, the role of the human resource department has been more to do with enforcing dictates from the top than with developing employees as individuals, growing the company's human capabilities. However, concepts and theories concerned with human behaviour—such as well-being, emotional intelligence, engagement, and creativity—are gradually being recognised as having an impact on the balance sheet, and are therefore becoming more familiar in the workplace, with soft skills playing a larger role in workforce and leadership development. Nevertheless, this movement has only just begun; the pre-eminence of left focus still holds sway, and although business is starting to recognise the benefits of right focus, it has not yet adapted to accommodate or encourage it.

My point is not that "people are cool," "people are important." It is that ... "people" (their talent, their creativity, their intellectual capital, their entrepreneurial drive) is all the hell there is.

TOM PETERS

Jazz-leadership breaks through the barrier of right focus by using structured approaches to make the system servant not master, to allow imagination to become productive, to hold activity rather than direct it, to bring clarity and provide security.

Form is possibility.

CECIL TAYLOR

142

FREEDOM WITH RESPONSIBILITY

All successful organisations have grown by implementing effective systems and processes; without them it's impossible to flourish. However, in these times of seismic change, the shape of organisations is morphing, and existing structures are rapidly becoming outmoded, with those needed to overcome right focus not yet fully formed. Rather than rebuilding from the rubble, organisations need a radically new approach to structure, or they will waste human capital, stultify creativity, halt innovation, and find employees increasingly disengaged, dissatisfied, and risk-averse.

> *As the painter needs his framework of parchment, the improvising musical group needs its framework in time.*
>
> BILL EVANS

Jazz has wrongly earned the reputation of being run along right focus lines—all imagination and no structure; possibly the roots of this lie in society's attitude to artists in general, and to the jazz musician in particular. However, if one examines the practicalities of being in the profession, it becomes apparent that many assumptions are based on ignorance of the facts, and a lack of understanding of a lifestyle that is, ironically, becoming increasingly common.

The reality of being a jazz musician begins with the same challenges encountered by the ever-increasing numbers of self-employed people, and struggled with by many who are unexpectedly thrust into an alternative work style, due to, for example, lay-offs, redundancy, flexible, part-time, or contract working.

Time management, along with self-motivation and good organisational abilities, are fundamental when you've nobody either setting your schedule, or holding you to it. The ability to structure the days, weeks, months, years of a career are entirely in the jazz musician's hands; they must organise a widely varied schedule, network and negotiate to secure work, plan and execute continuous learning, define specific tasks, and deal with ever-changing circumstances. Over-arching this day-to-day administration they must construct and maintain a career vision, and refer to this with each decision they make. Jazz improvisation is a way of life that combines unrelenting artistic demands with an unconditional requirement to self-manage—for the freedom to exist, it's necessary to create the structures within which it can take place.

It's a hard life out here. You have to be strong, you have to be organised, you got to be on top of a lot of stuff.
JOE LOVANO

Just as the jazz lifestyle can be misinterpreted, so can the jazz process. To the casual observer, improvisation can seem like a random, instinctive form of self-expression. In fact, the structure within which improvisation takes place is a model for overcoming right focus. Bill Evans called this, "freedom with responsibility," elaborating the idea by saying that however far he diverged or found freedom with the format, it's only free in so far as it has reference to the strictness of the original form; "and that's what gives it its strength."

In contrast to the traditional business approach, where left focus directs all action to the exclusion of right focus, jazz uses a union between left and right focus—left-focus 'logic' guiding the framework within which right-focus 'imagination' takes place. The structure constrains but does not dictate to the imagination—rather it's the canvas upon which the imagination turns into form.

Improvisation is a balance between control and surrender. It's like two sides of a highway. And you've got to walk down that yellow line.
BOBBY MCFERRIN

The structures used by the jazz-leader vary in complexity, and are chosen according to the context. For example, there are certain musical forms that every jazz musician learns, enabling a pick-up band to use these simple conventions in order to play together, to 'jam' in a coordinated way, or to perform without having previously met. These guiding structures are non-negotiable and impersonal, so players know exactly where they're meant to be, according to their role, and to what extent and when the given material can be transformed. Groups with a stable line-up can develop elaborate arrangements of their repertoire over time and, as musical personalities get better acquainted with each other, the adaptations during performance can become more sophisticated and spontaneous.

The Messengers use many devices to structure their arrangements while still leaving large, free spaces for blowing. The scores include interludes, tempo changes, and contrapuntal lines.

HORACE SILVER

The space for improvising, or 'blowing,' is the place where each individual can have their own voice heard, getting inspiration not only from their own imagination, but also drawing on the material contained in the pre-determined elements, as well as responding to others' ideas.

Composers and arrangers have great scope, in terms of structure, from rough sketches through to highly organised work. But whatever the structure, these compositions and arrangements provide the constraints for the improvisers, the secure elements within which the uncertainty takes place, the construct within which the imagination takes flight, the means of reducing some risk within an inherently risky environment.

146

Jazz is a very structured thing that comes down from a tradition and requires a lot of thought and study.

WYNTON MARSALIS

The jazz-leader is responsible for establishing this structure, providing guidelines that encourage appropriate risk-taking, and allowing each member to express themselves. Within this organised context, the work is shaped by the group, to evolve into an 'idea in the middle'—something created by everyone involved, that's born of, yet beyond, an original vision.

This approach to structure doesn't merely anticipate change, but requires it. All members share a mutual orientation, while being prepared to both lead and to follow, alert to the unexpected from themselves and others. Consequently, everyone is fully engaged, ready to respond to others' directions, expected to contribute their own perspective, to take risks, and to do it all in real time.

In organisations, structures are usually regulated by control mechanisms designed to minimise mistakes, which invariably deter risk-taking of any kind. While it's necessary to curtail foolish risks, this must not eliminate the risk-taking that's necessary for innovation and growth. There are various debates about how this can be achieved; at Davos 2012 the conclusion was that a 'control and collaborate' leadership model was needed, akin to the ambidextrous company proposed by Tushman and O'Reilly, which relies on a leader who is capable of this duality in approach. Charles O'Reilly described this as "managers who can simultaneously juggle several inconsistent organizational structures and cultures and who can build and maintain ambidextrous organizations."

The jazz-leadership model uses elements of 'control and collaborate', but in a way that is more integrated, less inconsistent—that is, there is no conflict between the structure and the freedom within it. Whatever the design, the structure is in a supporting role, one that holds change, and enables improvisation. In a large organisation this might entail small divisions or units, each with a bespoke structure according to their function, within which a jazz-leader holds the vision and provides the right environment for individual growth, purpose and autonomy, which produces peak group performance. For example, when Google teams come together to work on a particular project, each is assigned a leader whose role is not to direct action, but to support members, to help carry the project forward by addressing any problems, to arrange for the project's promotion within the organisation, and to guide and assist whenever possible.

The old model of the heroic superman is increasingly archaic. The most active and successful leaders today see themselves as part of the global community and peer groups. They listen as well as they speak. Never confuse charisma with leadership.

SAM PALMISANO

IBM's recently retired CEO, Sam Palmisano, recognised that the company's traditional command and control culture would not work in the twenty-first century. In 2003 he undertook a massive reorganisation, transforming the 440,000 employees in 170 countries into an 'integrated global enterprise,' which removed the old silos, and transformed the culture into a unique collaborative enterprise. Meanwhile, the hierarchical structure dominates in most organisations—an extension of the pervasive and persistent assumption that employees fall within McGregor's Theory X; that is, lacking personal motivation they need to be forced to work with the use of sticks and carrots. Consequently, goals are often over-prescriptive, motivation is extrinsic, strategy lacks flexibility, and teams are insufficiently aligned, so members are unable to adapt rapidly to each other's ideas.

The structure favoured by jazz-leaders promotes, rather than leaks, creativity; it encourages the individual to seek self-actualisation within a collaborative environment, and it not merely allows risk-taking—or improvising—but expects it.

Economic progress can be defined as the ability to take greater risks. The attempt to eliminate risks, even the attempt to minimize them, can only make them irrational and unbearable. It can only result in that greatest risk of all: rigidity.

PETER DRUCKER

Rules and Roles

The jazz-leadership approach to structure is built on the understanding that each individual is hired because they possess the necessary hard skills—knowledge and technical aptitude—to participate in a particular situation, within a specific role. Their suitability is based on their understanding of the rules of theory, the traditional structures, and the features of the particular style that the group works within. After theoretical knowledge comes their technical expertise, and their ability relative to the group's need. And then, beyond this, is the way they use these skills to express themselves—their individual interpretation of all the elements, and their ability to improvise. In addition to the hard skills associated with playing their instrument, the improviser needs the entire range of soft skills in order to be able to adapt to the culture of the particular group, to cope well with the pressures of practice and performance, and to navigate the practicalities of working within an uncertain environment.

Finding the right guys is really the hardest part of being leader. The rest gets to be largely routine and resigning yourself to being a bad guy part of the time. And a certain amount of patience, fortitude, and delicate negotiation is necessary.

PAUL DESMOND

'Finding the right guys' is in itself a compositional act, requiring the jazz-leader to recruit members who are technically and idiomatically capable of realising the vision, with musical and personal chemistry that suits the group, and who also have the necessary soft skills. This is crucial for the success of the organisation, and pivotal in developing an engaged workforce.

Recruiting is indeed the magic formula. It's how you get people you can bet the business on ... one bad hire is toxic.

JIM STENGEL

Companies with highly engaged employees are shown to achieve significantly better financial performance; research from Towers Watson shows that it produces around 3.5 per cent difference in net profits. Gallup recently estimated that the cost of disengaged workers in the U.S.A. is more than $300 billion in lost productivity alone. Meanwhile, many employees are disengaged; according of a study of 2000 organisations in 88 countries undertaken by the Hay group, HR managers believe employee motivation and engagement is their number one problem. However, disengagement can be turned around when a leader takes a genuine, active, and visible interest in their people. When Doug Conant took on the role of CEO of the Campbell Soup Company he found that 6000 of the 14,000 people working there were looking for jobs elsewhere. Tackling this as a priority, he reduced the ratio to 17 people engaged for every one that wasn't.

You cannot expect to perform at a high level unless people are personally engaged. And they're not going to be personally engaged unless they believe that you're personally engaged in trying to make their lives better.

DOUG CONANT

Problems with employee engagement are not always the result of poor leadership or an ineffective recruitment process, but can also be attributed to a lack of suitable applicants. A recent study by Leadership IQ tracked 20,000 new hires over a 3-year period—46 per cent failed within 18 months, a remarkably high figure which is nevertheless consistent with other studies. It showed that 89 per cent of failures were not due to lack of work skills in new recruits, but lack of soft skills—including motivation, attitude, emotional intelligence, and coachability. These results are similar to those produced by The Centre for Creative Leadership, which showed the primary causes of derailment in executives to be insufficient team-working capabilities, poor interpersonal relations, and difficulties in handling change; or the recent survey of Fortune 500 CEOs by Stanford Research Institute, which found that 75 per cent of long-term job success depends on soft skills and only 25 per cent on hard skills. The evidence is clear: whereas once an employee was expected merely to have the technical skills to undertake their job, this is no longer the case. Today's employees, at every level, need the same soft skills as jazz musicians, in order to cope with constant change, to work in teams, to be self-motivated, to be networked, and to improvise.

I'd rather hire a jazz musician, a dancer, or a captain in the Israeli army. They can learn about banking. It's much harder for bankers to unlearn their bad habits.

ARKADI KUHLMANN

Soft skills also have a part to play in the other side of the recruitment process; recruiters who have high soft-skills levels, particularly in the area of self-awareness, are more conscious of their own weaknesses, and have been shown to be better at hiring subordinates who perform well in areas where they themselves lack acumen. The knock-on effect of this is substantial; the U.S. Air Force found that the most successful recruiters scored significantly higher in the competencies of assertiveness, empathy, happiness, and emotional self-awareness. The immediate gain was judged to be a saving of $3 million annually.

The question is whether we have enough commitment to exercise the basics. One has to become humble in heart, in order to realize that there are secrets in the basics.

ABDULLAN IBRAHIM

So for improvisation to work well, each participant must have the necessary knowledge, technique, interpretive ability, and soft skills capability. In addition, they need a complete understanding of rules that govern group interplay and the ability to execute them automatically; at the centre of these is their role, along with its responsibilities. As with many aspects of jazz, there are clear guidelines here; everyone has a specific job to do, and it is accepted because it permits both the independence and the interdependence of players. These are the rules of engagement, providing an agreed framework for experimentation, and laying the foundation from which the necessary empathy and trust between players can develop.

I want to be involved with my own musical problems, so I expect the others in the group to be attuned to me, and to know instinctively what their role is.

BILL EVANS

Taking the bass and drums as examples, these instruments have a collective function as part of the rhythm section, in addition to their individual roles as both accompanists and soloists. Together they provide the anchor for the group, keeping the tempo steady, marking the structure, interjecting punctuation, responding to soloists. They work closely together, sometimes trading off the responsibility with each other, so if one gets freer then the other will be more constrained. But then they have their separate responsibilities as accompanists. "Bass means foundation" says Matt Hinton, "and bass players realise that their first job is to support the musicians and the ensemble." He believes that bass players know more about sharing and appreciating one another than any other musician. Dave Holland sees his position as "a tremendous responsibility to create a centre," while for saxophonist Branford Marsalis, "the basis of the whole thing is the bass player."

The drum is the heartbeat.

ROY HAYNES

Musicians talk about the drums as being the heart, the beat, the pulse that controls everything that happens. Louie Bellson believed that "drummers are the tone of life. We are rhythm, we are timing, we are pacing." For Jack de Johnette it's about laying down the groove and embellishing it, about "shifting, making subtle changes, stoking the fire, putting colours to it." The drums drive and decorate, laying down the pulse that underpins the group's activity, providing an embellished consistency that enables uncertainty, allowing the players to improvise on a secure basis. Jazz musicians intimately understand the role they play, and they are also entirely in tune with those that others play.

Just as you can learn to feel the rhythm of dance and song, you can learn to feel the rhythm of business.

ROTTENBERG AND SHUMAN

In many organisations, not only are one's own roles and responsibilities unclear, but those of others are too often a mystery, or misunderstood. For real engagement it's vital that people understand their role—not only what they do, but why it's important to the ensemble. At Michelin, an organisation of 115,000 employees, every individual knows what they're doing, why they're doing it, and, because they have a career manager, how their work today relates to their future. Michelin considers each person to be a "unique and irreplaceable asset, with emotions, capable of making decisions and progressing when given a chance."

The approach Michelin takes is not a nicety to the employees; it's sensible business. How can an employee have a sense of responsibility if they're unsure of their purpose? How can they be passionate about their work if they've no idea why their role matters, or how others rely on them? How can they feel part of something larger if they're not in touch with the whole ensemble? How can they be confident players if the rhythm of the business is unsteady? Michelin's policy of helping people "become what they are" rewards the company with unrivalled loyalty from their employees.

You not only have to know your own instrument, you must know the others and how to back them up at all times. That's jazz.

OSCAR PETERSON

CLARITY AND SIMPLICITY

Working well with others doesn't happen easily or quickly; it's the leader's responsibility to create the right environment for this to happen. The jazz-leader knows that their role is to bring clarity. Firstly, to ensure that everyone understands what is trying to be achieved—the vision and the strategy through which it will be realised. Then to provide the framework within which the necessary work can take place. And finally, to define the roles and responsibilities of everyone involved. Ensuring clarity in each dimension means people don't waste energy trying to figure out the mechanism, but can get on with the job of working together effectively.

> *The hardest thing for a musician to learn is how to play with people. That's what made the Basie rhythm section.*
>
> JO JONES

When jazz musicians talk about their role and responsibilities it's clear that they not only understand them but are passionate about them, and endeavour to carry them out to the best of their ability—for their own sense of worth, for the benefit of the group, and for the end result, the performance. This emotional connection to the work can only happen when there is clarity in the structure, when the uncertainty of 'what am I meant to be doing?' has been removed and the entire concentration is freed up into the service of the work in hand. Once structures have been agreed and understood by everyone, expectations have been clarified, and everyone's roles and responsibilities are known, then attention can be devoted to the work and not to the mechanics of it. In other words, clarity of structure enables freedom within it.

The qualities in music which I considered most important—and still do—were beauty, simplicity, originality, discrimination, and sincerity.
PAUL DESMOND

"It is about being very human in the world—making things simple, respecting and caring," was one of the new values produced by all Nokia employees when Jorma Ollila instigated the World Café methodology across Nokia. This successful consultation process produced compelling and original values, got all 'Nokians' intellectually engaged, connected, and understanding each other, and meant that, even during inevitable times of uncertainty, they would be a more cohesive team. The value of simplicity expressed by Nokia's employees is one shared by jazz-leaders, who believe that structure is more practical, and content more profound, when simplicity is achieved in both. Horace Silver realised that he could play less, that he could cut out notes and it would still be meaningful and beautiful, although "simplicity," as he says, "is very difficult." "No matter how simple it is, doing it from intention," is Steve Gadd's way of getting a particular kind of intensity. And Sonny Rollins espouses the process of developing a simple idea—taking it through "difficult waters," while maintaining this basic simplicity. These musicians are technically capable of producing extraordinarily complicated work, but they understand that the challenge is to remove the superfluous, and to state things as clearly as possible.

Making the simple complicated is commonplace; making the complicated simple, awesomely simple, that's creativity.

CHARLES MINGUS

Jean-Marie Dru takes Mingus's sentiment even further: "the ultimate skill in life consists in making complexity simple." Yet so many organisations have systems and policies that are unwieldy and burdensome, and that determine rather than support behaviour. Such structures don't recognise or respect other ways of working, cause deadlines to be missed and agreements to be broken, are enervating for employees, unproductive in terms of innovation, and generally inefficient.

Notation can be used as a point of reference, but the notation does not indicate music. It indicates a direction.

CECIL TAYLOR

ENVIRONMENT AND PERSONAL SPACE

Some organisations have established structures intended to encourage soft skills such as creativity, communication, team-working and collaboration. But too often these have been developed from a left-focus perspective, and are an adaptation to accommodate, rather than a design built from a radically different outlook for an entirely new purpose. Consequently, these structures are not producing the necessary results, and need to be reconsidered. For example, there's a widely accepted view that collaboration is the way forward for innovation, and that working alone is not only less effective, but something that people don't enjoy. This rationale has been used to support numerous strategies, including the extensive implementation of the open-plan office environment. Meanwhile, as far back as 1998, research has shown that open-plan offices reduce the productivity of knowledge workers by 66 per cent. A recent study by Dr Vinesh Oommen shows that 90 per cent of the time the outcome of working in an open-plan environment is negative, causing stress, conflict, and staff turnover. The reason for this can be explained in part by Dr Jack Lewis's work, which demonstrates that the brain responds to even relatively benign distractions, such as other people's conversations, with intense bursts that destroy concentration; research by Gloria Mark concluded that workers are interrupted every 11 minutes, on average, and it takes the same workers 25 minutes to return to the original task. Such findings will be of little surprise to the people expected to work in an open-plan environment, regardless of their task or their preference, and who find it disturbing. Many leaders continue buying into this design, and although it makes sense to a short-term bottom-line decision-making process, the damage to productivity and morale over the longer term need to be factored in before that decision can be rationalised.

We believe strongly that the nature of a person's work should dictate decisions about space — in other words, form should follow function.
NICK MACPHEE

There's evidence, including work by Mihaly Csikszentmihalyi and Gregory Feist, to show that much creative work is best done alone, that people enjoy privacy and are most productive when free from interruption. Psychologist Anders Eriksson found that the optimum way to master a field is to undertake "deliberate practice;" that is working, usually by oneself, on the task that's most demanding for you personally. And, "there are no shortcuts to gaining true expertise." Certainly jazz musicians, like many artists, spend a great deal of time in solitary practice, and often this is not merely to become an expert—which Eriksson estimated to take at least 10,000 hours—but because it is their favourite way of working.

Despite the fact that I am a professional performer, it is true that I have always preferred playing without an audience.

BILL EVANS

While collaboration is currently in favour as the best route to creativity, there are also many studies to show that working alone, in quiet, away from distraction, produces better results and improves well-being. This more introverted perspective is paid little attention in the work environment, yet there are many successful people in the world of business who call themselves introverts—highly effective collaborators who nevertheless have a preference for solitude, and need it in order to be creative. These reserved luminaries include Bill Gates, Warren Buffett, Katharine Graham, Charles Schwab, and Steve Wozniak.

Most inventors and engineers I've met are like me … they live in their heads. They are almost like artists. In fact the very best of them are artists. And artists work best alone.

STEVE WOZNIAK

If maximum creativity and best performance is to be achieved by all employees, then structures should not assume that everyone is, or should be, an extravert. The design of office environments needs to learn from the likes of Apple, whose Pixar building is designed to allow people their own space to work within and to find quiet when they need it, while a large central atrium encourages spontaneous meetings and conversation—locating toilets in that area guarantees everyone will go through it regularly and randomly. At Google there are numerous workspace options—from familiar open plan, to informal seating in the large corridors, or single-person booths, where employees can drop in for half an hour (the sign reads, "No camping allowed") to get some privacy for a phone call or quiet work.

Start thinking of solitude as a good thing. We're so busy communicating we don't have time to think—we don't have time to talk about the things that really matter.
SHERRY TURKLE

Similarly, brainstorming has found favour as the way to generate creative ideas, but according to Keith Sawyer, a psychologist at Washington University, "decades of research have consistently shown that brainstorming groups think of far fewer ideas than the same number of people who work alone and later pool their ideas." This chimes with the jazz approach, which expects each individual to work extensively and regularly on their own before collaborating with others.

The thing that all of us have given to ourselves and the rest of the world is hard work. Everyone has given time to develop on that instrument.
MAX ROACH

One of the instructions issued before a brainstorming session, and essential to the concept, is to suspend all judgement about ideas. While this does reduce conflict and elicits many ideas, there is conjecture that it favours quantity over quality. Improvisers have a different approach. They generate and explore numerous ideas, and in doing so are supported by the other participants, but these ideas are judged during the process, in so far as they will be adopted or rejected as a matter of course. The inherent weeding out of ideas determines which are weak and which merit further development.

Jazz means working things out with other people. You have to listen to other musicians and play with them even if you don't agree with what they're playing.

WYNTON MARSALIS

This evolution of ideas during improvisation precludes the 'groupthink' that can happen during brainstorming sessions—where peer pressure forces an idea through, not because of its inherent value, but because it's proposed by a charismatic individual, or appeals to the majority, thereby excluding the more introverted members, as well as the more unusual or challenging concepts. During an improvisation each member has their say, their solo; no matter how extravert or introvert, every individual will speak, and the others will listen and respond.

A good quartet is like a good conversation among friends interacting to each other's ideas.

STAN GETZ

SECURITY

For the jazz musician to perform, to improvise and to solo at their peak, they need to be certain that the structure they're working within is secure, that the functional elements are in place around them. In practice, this means that they understand and are confident about the arrangement of the music itself, that the pulse they're playing on is regular, and that the other musicians are capable, empathic, and reliable. With this framework providing the security they have space within which to experiment. In an organisation this equates to a working environment where employees can concentrate as well as collaborate, where they're treated in a consistent and respectful way, where expectations are clear, and where the systems, as well as colleagues, are supportive.

Leadership is about creating a domain in which human beings continually deepen their understanding of reality and become more capable of participating in the unfolding of the world.

PETER SENGE

When the functional processes are in place, the structure is unambiguous, roles and responsibilities are understood, individuals are trusted to prepare adequately and consistently for solo and group activity, and the vision and values are shared, then it's possible to hold ambiguity, to experiment and take risks, to allow paradox, uncertainty, friction, and to achieve peak individual, team, and organisational performance. This provides both a functional and a psychological security. The balance between structure and freedom, between autonomy and interplay, between leadership and followership, establishes an environment where personal engagement can combine with commitment to the group—and produce peak performance.

Something fresh will come up which you didn't even know you could play. That's what playing is really all about, the magic that happens when you least expect it.

BOBBY ROGOVIN

RIGHT FOCUS—NOTES

Using structured approaches, a jazz-leader:

- makes the system servant, not master
- designs strong, clear, impersonal frameworks
- enables freedom within agreed rules of engagement
- expects creativity, improvisation, and contribution
- ensures all roles and responsibilities are understood
- recruits for hard and soft skills equally
- designs space for solitude and for collaboration
- enables imagination to become productive
- strives for simplicity in everything
- creates a place of functional and psychological security.

CHAPTER 6

UPWARD FOCUS:
INSPIRATION<PURPOSE

F or an improviser, the years of study, practice, and performance are not merely to make a living; they're to achieve those occasional states that are glimpsed from time to time, where you're completely 'on purpose,' when you feel utterly free, when, as Art Farmer describes it —along with many others—"you forget yourself, you get to the point where the music doesn't come from you, it comes through you." The jazz-leader knows that this state of being on purpose is what motivates all improvisers. In fact, it's the state of self-actualisation that motivates all humans. And it can be achieved through any work, if the culture enables it, and the conditions and environment are set up for it.

Consequently, it's impossible to fully consider peak performance without recognising the part that upward focus plays. It is an essential part of performance at the highest level, of 'flow'—described by Csikszentmihalyi as our experience of optimal fulfilment and engagement—and of the transcendent experience that is the fundamental reward for playing jazz. This state of peak performance, which can be achieved through many human endeavours, including jazz and engaging work, is the most powerful motivator. Once an improviser has achieved this extraordinary state, and has experienced music being composed through them rather than by them, they willingly spend the rest of their lives in its service.

It's exhilarating and ecstatic, where you really get beyond yourself, and lose the positional boundaries of who you are and become merged with this marvellous experience.

DANNY ZEITLIN

Particularly in Western culture we have, by and large, externalised spirituality, and while it could be argued that it's central to every aspect of human existence, discussion about it is a complete anathema to the world of commerce. While religious beliefs are generally accepted and sometimes accommodated in the workplace, most people feel uncomfortable discussing a spiritual dimension of life in that context and few see its relevance to business. Consequently, upward focus, the sixth focus, is absent in most professional lives. BBM reflects this, and upward focus is treated differently to the other five focuses, not because it is less important, but because we currently have to function in an environment that gives it no consideration.

People create barriers between each other … when these barriers have been dissolved there arises one mind, where they are all one unit, but each person also retains his or her own individual awareness.

JOSEPH JAWORSKI

As with all the focuses, upward focus can become a barrier when its dominant influence draws too much attention. The barrier of upward focus, with the dominant influence of inspiration, causes a loss of connection with reality, an addiction to the ecstatic, and the pursuit of a divine yet elusive experience, to the exclusion of everything and everybody else.

It can also be a barrier if the individual is unable to move from the elation of the experience, and successfully re-enter an atmosphere of normality without finding it dull and unstimulating. Just as people completing a successful project can unexpectedly find themselves feeling deflated and suffering a sense of loss, an improviser commonly needs a period of transition after a euphoric experience, so they can return to the day-to-day routine of life.

However, when upward focus is in balance, and the individual is 'grounded'—connected to reality—while also interwoven with this spiritual dimension, then the result is a transformative sense of personal freedom and purpose.

RELINQUISHING CONTROL

*Sometimes I'm able to step outside myself and hear what I'm playing. The
ideas just flow. The horn and I become one.*
SONNY ROLLINS

As a rule, improvisers—and jazz-leaders—know that this mysterious state is
beyond their control and cannot be forced; in fact, the more they try to force
it, the more it will elude them, producing tension that distracts concentration and blocks imagination, disabling the mind from being free. They know
that it's impossible to achieve peak performance consistently or predictably;
blocked times are guaranteed to happen, and improvisers learn to accept this
and to be patient.

*Sometimes you have days when you just don't feel right, like there's some
kind of congestion and the flow isn't there.*
TOMMY FLANAGAN

While forward focus, or flow, can be achieved to a degree without upward
focus, anyone who has come close to this state knows that when it occurs,

something outside their own will is in control. In fact, you have to be able to relinquish control in order for it to happen.

Once I start playing, the music takes over. I feel like it's coming through me, not from me.

DOTTIE DODGION

Whilst it would not be possible without the requisite degree of skills supporting it, peak performance will not happen if the cognitive processes that helped acquire those skills continue to analyse and dictate the action. It's a discipline that requires the performer not only to know their 'stuff,' but then to be aware that the mind and the world are not separate, to recognise that other realm when they enter into it, to be brave enough to let go of conscious control, and to calmly observe the action unfold before them.

[When I'm singing] what I'm doing is watching it happen as it happens. The moment I start thinking about what I'm doing, then I get lost.

BOBBY MCFERRIN

Without upward focus, good performance is achievable on a regular basis; *with* upward focus, peak performance happens sometimes, just enough to keep the improviser committed to excellence because they want to be prepared, equipped with the skills they'll need, open and ready for when they are taken into that other place.

> *There's a professional level of creativity that I can depend on which is satisfactory for public performance. But those other high levels that happen just occasionally are really thrilling. You don't know when the heck they're going to come. You can't try to do it. All you do is look for it and sometimes it happens.*
>
> BILL EVANS

PURPOSE AND PASSION

One of the main reasons people are so disenchanted with their work is the lack of purpose and meaning in it. This is particularly the case with top talent, who are driven by the opportunity to be part of something that matters beyond money and power, and with young people, who are showing extreme dissatisfaction and disengagement. Recent research shows that, after pay, purpose is the reason that employees are both attracted and loyal to an organisation—"employees are looking for companies that have more to offer, that they can have a real connection with," says Mairi Doyle of BUPA.

If you feel that the person leading an organisation has a real sense of purpose

it becomes much more tangible through that whole organisation.

MARTHA LANE FOX

Yet most business leaders pay scant attention to this aspect. And even when they do, they can find resistance and scepticism from those around them who are uncomfortable with such change. When Leif Johansson began a cultural transformation at Volvo he produced a guiding document that challenged the company's traditional behaviours; initially, the use of words such as 'passion' evoked a mixture of jokes and ridicule. But that changed—" this was a success because this was something that people had actually been longing for,"—confirming Johansson's belief that people need meaning in their work, and that, given a compelling purpose, they will be intrinsically motivated to work with passion in its service.

Because you never know when the revelations will come to you, you have

to practice every day.

BARRY HARRIS

This state of peak performance can happen through any work, yet is very rarely taken into consideration in organisations. The assumption persists that people

THE JAZZ OF BUSINESS

do not want to work, and therefore cannot achieve real personal satisfaction, let alone any transcendent experience, through it, particularly if that work is not, in itself, exciting. This is not the case; purpose and meaning can be found through doing any activity.

The work exists for the person as much as the person exists for the work.
ROBERT GREENLEAF

This attitude is an overhang from the mechanistic thinking of the industrial age—a left-focus emphasis that has yet to lose its grasp. And the pervasive leadership style is still inextricably linked to this, assuming the position of command and control over others, rather than being in the position of enabler.

Alternatively, the jazz-leader works with the natural human drive to seek self-actualisation, positioning it not at the top of the hierarchy of needs, not as something that can only be achieved after everything else is taken care of, as Maslow suggested, but in a far more fundamental position. This stance is redolent of Csikszentmihalyi's early observations of student artists, who became so involved in the process of painting that it, "overrides almost everything else, except maybe the need to eat and sleep and go to the bathroom."

The whole thing of being in music is not to control it but to be swept away by it. If you're swept away by it you can't wait to do it again.

BOBBY HUTCHERSON

Rather than ignoring this exhilaration that all humans get from self-actualisation, the jazz-leader capitalises on it, so they can guarantee regular top performance from their team, plus occasional peak performance, and a constant, self-motivated drive for excellence from everyone involved.

It happens maybe three or four times a year; you pick up the horn and everything comes out just right—feeling, range, speed—you know just what you want and you can get it. It's a mysterious thing.

RAY ELDRIDGE

The possibility that intense personal satisfaction could happen at any time can be built into any working situation, because below the surface of every routine activity, and for every human being, is the realm of deeper feelings. Working *with* those deeper feelings, rather than denying them, inspires enduring commitment and personal fulfilment for the individual, while improving performance for the whole.

Everybody can feel what each other is thinking. You breathe together, you swell together, you just do everything together, and a different aura comes over the room.

MELBA LISTON

When a team builds a groove together it's a powerful experience, forging a bond that no controlled team-building exercise can ever hope to achieve. The impact of an elevated performance creates a unity between individuals that diminishes personal differences, and gives a team a life of its own. After a peak performance experience, each individual is emotionally charged, connected to the others, and intrinsically motivated towards making it happen again. A jazz-leader recognises this, builds on it, keeps the momentum up, and ensures that the environment is conducive to it happening again. They design the circumstances for its reoccurrence to the best of their ability; however, they don't demand when it should happen—they understand that this is not within their control. They recognise, as does everyone who experiences it, that peak performance doesn't happen to order. But when a working environment promises that it could happen at any time, then everyone is committed and alert.

To hear it all simultaneously is one of the most divine experiences that you can have.

LEE KONITZ

THE REAL INCENTIVE

Most incentives at work are based on money, because this is seen as the primary human motivator, the optimum method of producing peak performance, the reward we all supposedly seek and understand to be the measure of success. But being a successful, fulfilled, happy person has been shown to have relatively little to do with the level of our financial wealth. Beyond a basic ability to comfortably pay our bills, our finances have been shown to have no effect on our overall well-being; research from Princeton University shows that an annual household income of $75,000 marks the point at which money will not affect happiness, and a recent Ipsos poll that surveyed 19,000 adults in 24 countries found the happiest were in poor and middle-income countries, while the gloomiest were in rich countries.

We have created a culture that's filled to the top with people that are using material good, commercialism, politics, and the economy to hide. What we have to figure out is how to strip away those hiding places, so we can actually do the important work.

CHIP CONLEY

While we have been led to believe that winning external rewards, particularly money, is the route to our happiness, it seems not to be the case. Instead happiness has far more to do with feeling that we have purpose, and that we're progressing in work that we find meaningful. Living and working from this stance means that we're more consistently happy, we're resilient, we willingly take on the challenges and problems encountered on our quest, we're intrinsically motivated, moved by our own spur, and we find reward in the process itself.

Music has allowed me to understand that success is everything that you are, more than what it is you've accomplished.

ORNETTE COLEMAN

The jazz-leader taps into this pool of the human spirit, often speaking in terms of the spiritual side of life when discussing their work. John Coltrane considered music to be a healing, uplifting art, a way of learning more about himself and his part in "the unity of all being," while Wayne Shorter believes that when an artist creates they "feed the soul, heal the soul, make the soul well."

It's like a preacher, in a sense. And the instrument, any instrument, shouldn't get in the way.

CHARLES MINGUS

Quincy Jones has an expression when recording: "leave God a little room to come through—give him 20 to 30% of the room," because "a lot of magic has to go down;" while for Cecil Taylor, "it's about magic and capturing spirits." Jimmy Heath believed that, "if you don't have the whole spiritual thing, I don't think jazz is complete;" and Stephane Grappelli saw jazz as music that "comes from the skies, from heaven, from God."

> *When the music's happening, I'm in love with the bass—and I'm in love with life.*
> DON PATE

The reward for playing jazz is, as John Lewis said, "playing jazz." The impossibility of the task, the insecurity of the career, the never-ending learning, the lack of societal appreciation, the musical frustrations, all these are worth it purely for those elusive, occasional times when the groove emerges, when, as Leroy Williams put it, "there's a feeling you just can't buy."

> *If the rhythm section is really swinging, it's such a great feeling, you just want to laugh.*
> EMILY REMLER

This feeling of living to the full in the moment is far more potent as a human motivator than any bonus or promotion, and can be built into *any* human activity. It's how the jazz-leader inspires and engages their people, how they incentivise them to be constantly intrinsically motivated, to achieve consistently good performance, to bond with others as a natural process of working together with the common desire of achieving the groove, to be committed to the process, and to occasionally hit the elusive peak performance which is the reward in itself. This way, jazz-leaders always get great, always make progress, and regularly achieve the extraordinary.

At the heart of jazz is the need to communicate, to be part of something greater than oneself, to reach some eternal values ... immutable values in the universe that we experience as often chaotic and full of change.

DANNY ZEITLIN

BIBLIOGRAPHY

Alkyer, F. & Enright, E. *Downbeat: The Great Jazz Interviews*. Hal Leonard Books, 2009.

Amabile, T.M. "Motivation and creativity: Effects of motivational orientation on creative writers." *Journal of Personality and Social Psychology, 48*(2), 393–397, 1985.

Amabile, T.M. & Kramer, S.J. *The Progress Principle: Using Small Wins to Ignite Joy, Engagement, and Creativity at Work*. Harvard Business Review Press, 2011.

Argyris, C. *On Organizational Learning*. Blackwell, 1992.

Argyris, C. *"Initiating change that perseveres." American Behavioral Scientist*, 40(3), 299–309, 1997.

Banbury, S. & Berry, D. "Disruption of office-related tasks by speech and office noise." *British Journal of Psychology*, 89: 499–517, 1998.

Barrett, F.J. "Creativity and improvisation in jazz and organizations: Implications for organizational learning." *Organization Science, 9*, 558–560, 1998.

Bennis, W. *Flight Plan for Leaders: or the Puck, the Plaque and the Art of Jazz*. USC Business, 1994.

Berendt, J. *The Jazz Book*. Granada Publishing, 1976.

Berliner, P.F. *Thinking in Jazz: The Infinite Art of Improvisation*. The University of Chicago Press, 1994.

Bernstein, E.S & Barrett, F.J. "Jazz mindset: exploring practices that enhance dynamic capabilities for organizational improvisation." *Research in Organizational Change and Development*, Volume 19, 55–90, Emerald Group Publishing Ltd, 2011.

Blanchard, K. *Leading at a Higher Level*. Pearson Education, 2010.

Bohm, D. *On Dialogue*, David Bohm Seminars, 1990.

Brown, A.D. & Thornborrow, W.T. "Do organizations get the followers they deserve?" *Leadership & Organization Development Journal*, 17, 5–11. 1996.

Buber, M. *I and Thou*. Simon Schuster, 1970.

Burnison, G. *No Fear of Failure: Real Stories of How Leaders Deal With Risk and Change*. John Wiley & Sons, 2011.

Calling Brands. *Crunch Time: Why We Need Purpose at Work*. Engine Partners UK LLP, 2012.

Carter, N.M. & Wagner, H.M. *The Bottom Line: Corporate Performance and Women's Representation on Boards (2004–2008)*. Catalyst, March 2011.

Cartwright, R. *Mastering Team Leadership*. Palgrave Macmillan, 2002.

Cho, A. *The Jazz Process: Collaboration, Innovation & Agility*. Pearson Education. 2010.

Collier, J.L. *The Making of Jazz: A Comprehensive History*. Granada Publishing, 1978.

Collins, J. *Good to Great*. Harper Business, 2001.

Covey, S. *The Speed of Trust: The One Thing That Changes Everything*. Free Press, 2006.

Criswell, C. & Martin, A. *10 trends*. Center for Creative Leadership, 2007.

Crouch, S. *Considering Genius: Writings on Jazz*. Basic Civitas Books, 2006.

Csikszentmihalyi, M. *Good Business: Leadership, Flow, and the Making of Meaning*. Penguin, 2003.

Debold, E. "Flow with Soul: interview with Dr Mihaly Csikszentmihalyi." *EnlightenNext Magazine*, Spring–Summer 2002.

De Bono, E. *New Thinking for the New Millennium*. Penguin, 2000.

Denning, S. *The Secret Language of Leadership: How Leaders Inspire Action Through Narrative*. John Wiley & Sons, 2007.

De Haan, E. *Development at the Top: Who Really Cares? A Survey of Executive Teams.* Ashridge Business School, 2010.

DePree, M. *Leadership Jazz.* Dell Publishing, 1993.

Disruptive Innovation Explained: Interview with Clay Christensen. Video. HBR Blog Network. March 6, 2012.

D'Mello, S. *Stress: The Global Economic Downturn Has Taken Its Toll on Employees. What's the Impact for Organizations?* Kenexa High Performance Institute, 2012.

Dotlich, D.L. & Noel, J.L. *Action Learning: How the World's Top Companies Are Re-Creating Their Leaders and Themselves.* Jossey-Bass, 1998.

Dru, J,M. *Beyond Disruption:Changing the Rules in the Marketplace.* John Wiley & Sons, 2002.

Dru, J.M. *How Disruption Brought Order.* Palgrave Macmillan, 2007.

Drucker, P. *Managing in a Time of Great Change.* Truman Talley Books, 1995.

Enriquez, J. *As the Future Catches You: How Genomics & Other Forces are Changing Your Life, Work, Health & Wealth.* Three Rivers Press, 2001.

Ericsson, K. A., Prietula, M. J. & Cokely, E.T. *The Making of an Expert.* Harvard Business School, 2007.

Evans, B. *Liner Notes to Kind of Blue by Miles Davis.* Columbia Records, 1959.

Evans, B. *The Universal Mind of Bill Evans.* DVD. Discovery Records. 2005.

Evans, B. *Bill Evans Trio in Helsinki* 1970. DVD. Jazz Shots Spain, 2009.

Foster, R. & Kaplan, S. *Creative Destruction: Why Companies That Are Built to Last Underperform the Market—and How to Successfully Transform Them.* Doubleday, 2001.

George, Bill. *The Journey to Authenticity.* Leader to Leader Institute, Winter 2004.

Gitsham, A. et al. *Developing the Global Leader of Tomorrow.* Ashridge Business School, 2010.

Gladwell, M. *The Tipping Point.* Abacus, 2000.

Godin, S. *Linchpin: Are You Indispensable?* Piatkis, 2010.

Goleman, D. *Working with Emotional Intelligence.* Bloomsbury, 1998.

Goleman, D. *Social Intelligence.* Random House, 2006.

Goleman, D., Boyatzis, R. & McKee, A. *Primal Leadership.* Harvard Business School Press, 2002.

Goncalo, J. A., Flynn, F. J., & Kim, S. H. "Are two narcissists better than one?: The link between narcissism, perceived creativity and creative performance." *Personality and Social Psychology Bulletin*, 36, 1484–1495. 2010.

Grant, A.M. "Does intrinsic motivation fuel the prosocial fire? Motivational synergy in predicting persistence, performance, and productivity." *Journal of Applied Psychology*, 93(1), 48–58, 2008.

Greenleaf, R.K. *The Servant as Leader.* Robert K Greenleaf Center, 1982.

Hamel, G. *Leading the Revolution.* Harvard Business School Press, 2000.

Hamel, G. *The Future of Management.* Harvard Business School Press, 2007.

Handy, C. *Beyond Certainty.* Hutchinson, 1995.

Hentoff, N. & Shapiro, N. *The Jazz Makers.* Doubleday & Company, 1957.

Hentoff, N. *Jazz Is.* Random House, 1972.

Kao, J. *Jamming: the Art and Discipline of Business Creativity.* Harper Collins Business, 1997.

Kern, F. "What chief executives really want." *Bloomberg Businessweek*, May 2010.

House, R.J. & Howell, J.M. "Personality and charismatic leadership." *Leadership Quarterly. Special Issue: Individual differences and leadership: III*, 3(2), 81–108, 1992.

Humphreys, M., Ucbasaran, D. & Lockett, A. *Leading Entrepreneurial Teams: Insights from Jazz.* 33rd Institute for Small Business and Entrepreneurship Conference 2–4 November 2010.

Jaworski, J. *Synchronicity: The Inner Path of Leadership.* Berrett-Koehler, 1996.

Kelley, T. *The Art of Innovation*. Harper Collins Business, 2002.

Kolb, D. *Experiential Learning*. Prentice Hall, 1984.

Kouzes, J.M. & Posner, B.Z. *The Leadership Challenge*. John Wiley & Sons, Inc., 2007.

Lafley, A.G. & Charan, R. *The Game-Changer: How You Can Drive Revenue and Profit Growth with Innovation*. Crown Business, 2008.

Lehrer, J. "Groupthink: The brainstorming myth." *The New Yorker*, January 30, 2012.

MacAdams, L. *Birth of the Cool: Beat, Bebop & the American Avant-Garde*. Scribner, 2002.

MacPhee,N. & Vischer, J. "Will this open space work?" *Harvard Business Review,* May–June 1999.

Marsalis, W. *Moving to Higher Ground: How Jazz Can Change Your Life*. Random House, 2009.

Martin, M. *Meaningful Work: Rethinking Professional Ethics*. Oxford University Press, 2000.

Martin, R.L. *Fixing the Game: Bubbles, Crashes, and What Capitalism Can Learn from the NFL*. Harvard Business Review Press, May 2011.

Martineau, J.W. & Hannum, K.M. *Evaluating the Impact of Leadership Development: A Professional Guide*. Center for Creative Leadership, 2003.

McPartland, M. *Marian McPartland's Jazz World: All in Good Time*. University of Illinois Press, 2003.

Mingus, C. *Beneath the Underdog*. Payback Press, 1995.

Morrell, M. & Capparell, S. *Shackleton's Way*. Nicholas Brearley Publishing, 2001.

Moss Kanter, R. *The Change Masters*. ITP, 1983.

Mueller, J., Goncalo, J. and Kamdar, D. *Recognizing Creative Leadership: Can Creative Idea Expression Negatively Relate to Perceptions of Leadership Potential?* Cornell University, ILR School, 2010.

Mumford, M.D. & Connelly, M.S. "Leaders as creators: Leader performance and problem solving in ill-defined domains." *Leadership Quarterly. Special Issue: Individual differences and leadership: I,* 2(4), 289–315, 1991.

Murphy, M. *Hiring for Attitude: A Revolutionary Approach to Recruiting and Selecting People with Both Tremendous Skills and Superb Attitude.* McGraw-Hill, 2012.

Oommen, V.G., Knowles, M. & Zhao, I. "Should health service managers embrace open plan work environments? A review." *Asia-Pacific Journal of Health Management* 2008; 3:2.

Ordonez L.D. et al. *Goals Gone Wild: The Systematic Side Effects of Over-Prescribing Goal Setting.* Harvard Business School, 2009.

Parker, L. & Bevan, S. *Good Work and Our Times: Report of the Good Work Commission.* The Work Foundation, 2011.

Perspectives: Turbocharging Employee Engagement—the Power of Recognition from Managers. Towers Watson, 2010.

Peters, T. *Re-Imagine! Business Excellence in a Disruptive Age.* Dorling Kindersley, 2003.

Peters, T. *The Little Big Things: 163 Ways to Pursue Excellence.* Harper Collins, 2010.

Peters, T. *Off the Cuff #3.* Video. TomPeters! March 2012.

Petzinger, T. *The New Pioneers.* Touchstone, 1999.

Pine, B.J. & Gilmore, J.H. *The Experience Economy: Work is the Theatre and Every Business a Stage.* HBS Press, 1999.

Pink, D.H. *A Whole New Mind: How to Thrive in the New Conceptual Age.* Cyan, 2005.

Pink, D.H. *Drive: The Surprising Truth about What Motivates Us.* Video. RSA Animate, April 1, 2010.

Placksin, S. *Jazz Women 1900 to the Present: Their Words, Lives and Music.* Pluto Press, 1985.

Priest, S. *A Community First*. DaVita University, November, 2010.

Pulley, M.L. & Wakefield, M. *Building Resiliency: How to Survive in Times of Change*. Center for Creative Leadership, 2001.

Rath, T. & Conchie, B. *Strengths-based Leadership*. Gallup Press, 2008.

Ridderstrale, J. & Nordstrom, K. *Funky Business*. Pearson Education, 2000.

Rottenberg, D. & Shuman, J.C. *The Rhythm of Business: The Key to Building and Running Successful Companies*. Butterworth-Heinemann, 1998.

Scharmer, C.O. *Prescencing: Learning from the Future as it Emerges*. MIT Sloan School of Management Society for Organisational Learning, 2000.

Schuller, G. *Early Jazz: Its Roots and Musical Development*. Oxford University Press, 1968.

See, K.E., et al. "The Detrimental Effects of Power on Confidence, Advice Taking, and Accuracy." *Organizational Behavior and Human Decision Processes (2011)*, doi:10.1016/j.obhdp.2011.07.006

Senge, P.M. et al. *The Fifth Discipline Fieldbook. Strategies and Tools for Building a Learning Organization*. Doubleday, 1994.

Sidran, B. *Talking Jazz: An Oral History*. Da Capo Press, 1995.

Slattery C. *The Dark Side of Leadership: Troubling Times at the Top*. Semann & Slattery, 2009.

Spiro, L.N. "In search of leaders." *CEO Magazine*, October 2003.

Staw, B.M. "Is group creativity really an oxymoron." *Research on Managing Groups and Teams*. Volume 12, 311–323. Emerald Publishing Ltd. 2009.

Stengel, J. *Grow: How Ideals Power Growth and Profit at the World's 50 Greatest Companies*. Random House, 2011.

Stephenson, E. et al. "How Companies Act on Global Trends." *McKinsey quarterly*, April, 2008.

Thompson, C. "Meet the Life Hackers." *The New York Times*. October 16, 2005.

Tobin, P. *Barrier Breakers: Be Yourself Brilliantly!* Dodgem, 2010.

Tobin, P. *Managing Ourselves – Leading Others.* ICEL 2006 Inspiring Leadership: Experiential Learning and Leadership Development. Journal 12, 36–42. 2006.

Tobin, P. & Shrubshall, C. *How to Access and Manage Creativity in Organisations: A Collection of Perspectives.* RSA, 2002.

Tushman, M. & O'Reilly, C. *Winning through Innovation: A Practical Guide to Leading Organizational Change and Renewal.* Harvard Business School, 1997.

Uzzi, B. & Spiro, J. *Collaboration and Creativity: The Small World Problem.* University of Chicago, 2005.

Verma, S. "The softer side of management." *Businessworld*, May, 2012.

Wheatley, M.J. & Kellner-Rogers, M. *A Simpler Way.* Berrett-Koehler Publishers, 1996.

Why Diversity Matters: Research studies 2005–2010. Catalyst Information Center, November 2010.

Women Matter: Gender Diversity, a Corporate Performance Driver. McKinsey and Company, 2007.

Women Matter 2: Female Leadership, a Competitive Edge for the Future. McKinsey & Company, 2008.

Women Poised to Effectively Lead in Matrix Work Environments. Hay Group, March 27, 2012.

Wildermuth, C. *Voices of Leadership: Interview with Meg Wheatley.* www.criswildermuth.com, 2011.

Williams, M. *The Jazz Tradition.* Oxford University Press, 1983.

Willigan, G. Nokia: *Values That Make a Company Global.* Society for Human Resource Management, 2009.

Wilmer, V. *Jazz People.* Anchor Press, 1977.